A DICTIONARY OF
BRITISH ANIMAL PAINTERS

A Dictionary of

BRITISH ANIMAL PAINTERS

LIEUT. COLONEL J. C. WOOD

F. LEWIS, PUBLISHERS, LTD

PUBLISHERS BY APPOINTMENT TO THE LATE QUEEN MARY

The Tithe House, Leigh-on-Sea, England

SBN 85317 019 3

First Published 1973

Printed in Great Britain by
The Scolar Press, Ilkley, Yorkshire.

Foreword

It is eight years since Sydney Pavière's Dictionary of British Sporting Painters was published. During this time interest in Animal Painting, and particularly that of the Victorian era, has quickened. Little-known artists and long-forgotten pictures continue, and will continue, to emerge from obscurity so that no claim is made that this volume is definitive.

It is not intended to be the complement to the Dictionary of British Sporting Painters but to be a companion volume. The names of those sporting artists who were Animal Painters may be found in both volumes.

I have taken as my definition of an Animal Painter an artist who habitually made studies of, or painted portraits of, animals. This excludes, therefore, the many landscapists and pastoralists who, while making cattle the focal points of their compositions, did not paint them in detail; a few, such as Sydney Cooper who did so, are included. You will not find Gainsborough here nor Van Dyck included for the sake of his sitters' steeds; their fame does not rest on their having been Animal Painters. Neither have I included those artists – and they are not a few – who may have painted one picture of an animal amongst a large and varied output.

My thanks are due to many who have helped me with information for this compilation: in particular Messrs. A. Ackermann & Son Ltd., Messrs. Fores, Messrs. Oscar & Peter Johnson, the Moorland and the Tryon Galleries: they are not, of course, responsible for opinions expressed. I should like also to thank the Directors of many Provincial Museums and Art Galleries for their helpful replies to my enquiries.

My sources have been so numerous and varied that it is impossible to acknowledge them all. I should like, however, to express my gratitude to Christopher Wood whose comprehensive and detailed 'Dictionary of Victorian Painters' has recently filled a void in our knowledge about many painters working in this country during that era.

J. C. WOOD
1972

AUTHORITIES MENTIONED BY NAME IN THE TEXT

Gilbey	*Animal Painters of England* by Sir Walter Gilbey, Bart.
Grant	*A Dictionary of British Landscape Painters* by Col. M. H. Grant
Paget	*Sporting Pictures of England* by Guy Paget
Pavière	*A Dictionary of British Sporting Painters* by S. H. Pavière
Shaw Sparrow	*British Sporting Artists* and *A Book of Sporting Painters* by W. Shaw Sparrow
Walpole	*Anecdotes of Painting* by Horace Walpole, who incorporated in it the notes of George Vertue.

Abbreviations

A.G.	Art Gallery
A.R.A.	Associate of the Royal Academy
A.R.S.A.	Associate of the Royal Scottish Academy
b.	born
B.I.	British Institution
B.S.P.	Dictionary of British Sporting Painters
Coll :	Collection of
d.	died
D.N.B.	*Dictionary of National Biography*
F.S.	Free Society of Artists, 1760-1783
N.W.C.S.	New Water Colour Society
O.W.C.S.	Old Water Colour Society
op.	operating
P.R.A.	President of the Royal Academy
P.R.W.S.	President of the Royal Society of Painters in Water Colours
R.A.	Royal Academy or Royal Academician
R.B.A.	Member of the Royal Society of British Artists
R.H.A.	Royal Hibernian Society or member of same
R.I.	Royal Institute of Painters in Water Colours or member of same
R.O.I.	Royal Institute of Oil Painters
R.S.A.	Royal Scottish Academy or member of same
R.W.S.	Royal Society of Painters in Water Colours or member of same
s. & d.	Signed and dated
S.A.	Society of Artists, London, 1760-1791
S.S.	Suffolk Street Galleries; the Society of British Artists, 1824, became Royal in 1887.
B.M.	British Museum
Fitzwilliam	Fitzwilliam Museum, Cambridge
Nat. Gal.	National Gallery, London
Nat. Port. Gal.	National Portrait Gallery
Reading	Reading University Museum of Rural Life
Tate	Tate Gallery, London
Walker	Walker Art Gallery, Liverpool
V. & A.	Victoria & Albert Museum, London

ABBOTT, RICHMOND.   op. 1857-1866
He lived in Liverpool and at Wrexham. Cats and dogs were the subjects of his exhibited pictures.
He exhibited 3 works at B.I. and 4 at S.S.

ADAM, EMIL.   1843-1924
This German came to England in the 1880's and was commissioned by the Dukes of Portland and West-minster and other owners to portray their famous race-horses. He painted them in their loose-boxes with scientific accuracy, producing, before the era of colour photography, historical records of interest to students of bloodstock-breeding, if to few others.
There is a collection of these in the Jockey Club Rooms at Newmarket.

ADAM, JOSEPH DENOVAN, R.S.A., R.S.W.   1842-1896
The son of Joseph Adam, a landscapist, under whom he studied before going to the South Kensington Schools, he returned to Scotland and started a school of animal painting near Stirling. Like Louis Hurt, (q.v.), he delighted in painting Highland cattle, but placing them in bleaker settings than Hurt, he did not gain wide popularity.
He exhibited at R.A. from 1860-1892 and at B.I. and S.S.

*AGASSE, JAMES LAURENT.   1767-1849
British by adoption though a native of Geneva, at the beginning of the 19th century he came to London from Paris where he had worked under David and Horace Vernet and had studied anatomy at the Veter-inary College.
A true artist with his own individual style, he well deserved the high reputation that he gained. He did not restrict himself solely to portraits of horses and other animals, but painted scenes of sport and countryside with mastery. For George IV he painted 'The Nubian Giraffe' and 'White-tailed Gnus', still in the Royal Collection. He must be considered in the top rank of animal painters in the first half of the 19th century. Although held in high regard by his fellow artists, nevertheless he died in poverty.
He exhibited 29 works at the R.A., 7 at B.I., and 5 at S.S.
Coll : Royal Coll., Mellon Coll., and Geneva.

ALDIN, CECIL CHARLES WINDSOR.   1870-1935
Born at Slough, he studied art at South Kensington under Frank Calderon. Though primarily a sporting artist – he was an M.F.H. – his portrait drawings of dogs earned a wider popularity than his somewhat flat hunting scenes.
 He contributed regularly to sporting periodicals and published four illustrated books.

ALEXANDER, EDWIN, R.S.A.   1870-1928
Son of R. Alexander, he worked in oils and watercolours over a wide range, painting animals, birds and flowers. In his youth he visited Tangiers with his father and Joseph Crawhall (q.v.) who greatly influenced him. After studying in Paris he went to Egypt for 4 years and painted many Arab subjects. He became a member of the Glasgow Group of which Crawhall was the doyen. His watercolours were often painted on silk or linen. He became a full member of R.W.S. : he was made R.S.A. in 1913. He died at Musselburgh.
Coll : Glasgow, Belfast.

ALEXANDER, ROBERT, R.S.A., R.S.W.   1840-1923
Born at Dolgaren, Ayrshire, he was apprenticed to a Kilmarnock house painter who painted landscape. From 1868 he devoted himself to painting dogs and horses. He received commissions to paint bloodstock from such patrons as the Duke of Portland. He exhibited one picture at the R.A. in 1878.
Coll : The National Gallery at Edinburgh and Glasgow A.G.

ALKEN, GEORGE.   c. 1794 - c. 1837
The 3rd son of Samuel Alken, it seems likely that he was born in 1794/5, and died before 1837. A miniaturist and sporting painter, he produced a book of 47 lithographs in 1823, the subjects being studies of animals and sporting scenes, the quality fair. In 1827 he drew and aquatinted a set of St Leger Winners. He made many other sporting prints.

ALKEN, HENRY THOMAS.   1785-1851

Born in London, the 2nd son of Samuel Alken, he became the most famous of this family of sporting artists. His early training under his father and the miniaturist J. T. Barber is reflected in his best work; the figures are miniatures of living men and horses. In 1816 he produced a treatise on Horses, 'The Beauties and Defects in the Figure of the Horse comparatively delineated'. He went to Melton to hunt and draw, frequently introducing humour into his compositions. In later life the quality of his drawings and etchings deteriorated. His son Samuel Henry, an inferior artist, unscrupulously used his father's signature of 'H. Alken'.
Illustration in B.S.P.
Coll: Walker, V. & A.

ALKEN, SAMUEL.   1756-1815

Born in London, he was an architect and engraver. The father of four sporting artists, two of whom signed their work S. Alken at times, doubt exists as to whether he, himself, could thus be classified. Shaw Sparrow considered that mature work so signed and dated before 1804, when his son Samuel was only 20, can be ascribed to him with confidence.

ALKEN, SAMUEL, Jnr.   1784-1825

Born in London, the 1st son of Samuel Alken, he is believed to have died about 1825. He was primarily a sporting artist though portraits of horses are recorded from him.

ALKEN, SAMUEL HENRY.   1810-1894

The elder son of Henry Thomas Alken, he was born in Ipswich. He had talent as a sporting artist but unscrupulously signed his work H. Alken to pass it off as that of his father. He was also known as Henry 'Gordon' Alken in an attempt to distinguish him from his father. He lacked the delicacy of his father's touch.
Illustration in B.S.P.
Coll: Walker A.G.

ALKEN, SEFFREIN JOHN.   1796-1837

The youngest son of Samuel Alken, snr., he was, like his brothers, a sporting artist and also, like his eldest brother, signed his work S. Alken. Shaw Sparrow considered his signature to be smaller and neater than that of his brother.

ALKEN, SEFFERIN.   1821-1873

He was the 2nd son of Henry Thomas Alken and another of this family of sporting artists who signed his work S. Alken.

*ANSDELL, RICHARD, R.A.   1815-1885

Born and schooled in Liverpool, he studied art under W. C. Smith, a Chatham portrait painter. He became a prolific painter of animals and of Highland and Spanish scenes in the manner of Landseer: Grant considered his technique of colour and impasto to be superior. While Landseer loved to portray the intelligence of animals, regarded nowadays as sickly sentimentality, Ansdell had a wider range and was not afraid to show their fiercer qualities. At his best he must be considered in the front rank of 19th century animal painters. Although the figures predominate in his pictures, the surrounding landscape is equally well painted. He collaborated occasionally with Thomas Creswick, R.A., and etched a few plates of animals. In 1856 he visited Spain with John Philip with whom he worked. His large output was so appreciated in his lifetime that he was able to amass a fortune. He was a member of the Liverpool Academy and was elected President of it from 1837-1852.
He exhibited at the R.A. from 1840-1885.
Coll: The R.A., the Tate, the Walker, Manchester, Hull, Leeds, Cheltenham and Preston A.G's.
Illustration in B.S.P.

ANSELL, CHARLES.   op. 1780-1790

Six aquatints engraved by F. Jukes of this artist's 'Life of a Race-Horse' were published in 1784. This was a year after Thomas Gooch had exhibited his set in oils of the same subject at the R.A. and indicates that he cribbed this theme from Gooch. Sutherland engraved 10 of his hunting scenes and another large set, in which shooting predominates, in 1789, while P. W. Tompkins engraved many of his humorous domestic scenes.

ARGENT, —. op. 1782-1783

This early animal painter exhibited 3 pictures at the Free Society. Two were drawings of lions.

ARMFIELD, (Smith), GEORGE. *c.* 1808-1893

This minor but prolific artist gained early success with the public for his cheerful sporting pictures in which dogs were his favourite subjects. A keen sportsman and fine horseman with a passion for fox-hunting, he had a great love of animals over which he could exert an extraordinary influence. Until 1839 he exhibited under his family name as G. A. Smith, sending 5 works to R.A., 2 to B.I. and 1 to S.S.

From 1840 he dropped 'Smith' from his name. His best period is considered to be from then until 1869. A free spender, he was a rapid worker and had an enormous output: it is safe to say that no painter will exceed the number of his pictures of terriers ratting.

His prolificacy extended to his private life and of the dozen children of his 3rd marriage, another George, followed his progenitor's calling.

As Geo. Armfield he sent 32 works to R.A., 30 to B.I., and 41 to S.S.

Coll: The Walker and Glasgow A.G's.

ARMOUR, GEORGE DENHOLM, O.B.E. 1864-1949

After studying at the Edinburgh School of Art and the Royal Scottish Academy, in 1888 he went to London and worked as a painter and illustrator. For years he contributed to 'Punch' drawings of sporting and rustic humour, conveying most simply in his settings the usual wet and muddy conditions. He illustrated in colour – the paintings often on linen – two books on 'Jorrocks' and Beckford's 'Thoughts on Hunting', showing great talent in depicting both horses and hounds.

In his equestrian portraits, of which those of the Dowager Duchess of Beaufort, Sir Lionel Durell, and Captain Gerald Digby are examples, he could 'get' the characters of both horse and rider.

ATKINSON, JOHN AUGUSTUS, O.W.C.S. 1775-?1833

The outstanding quality of this London-born artist was his ability to convey movement, especially that of horses, in a picture. He worked in both oils and watercolour, in the latter with speed and lightness of touch. He is best known for his scenes in Russia where he lived from 1784-1801, and for his battle pieces of which the most famous was his 'Waterloo' shown at the R.A. in 1816.

He was prolific and exhibited in London from 1803-1833.

He exhibited 60 works at R.A., 41 at B.I., 24 at S.S., and 68 at O.W.C.S.

Coll: V. & A., Derby.

BACON, D'ARCY. op. 1855-1874

He painted animals and exhibited pictures such as 'The Haunt of the Heron' and the 'Haunt of the Red Deer'.

He exhibited 1 work at R.A., 3 at B.I., and 10 at S.S.

BAIRD, NATHANIEL HUGHES JOHN, R.O. 1854-1936

This Scot from Roxburghshire studied in Paris under Bouguereau and Duran before going to the Herkomer School at Bushey.

He painted portraits, landscape, and rural scenes with animals. In the 1880's he published 'Antiquities of Exeter' which were reproduced by J. G. Commin: the originals were acquired by the V. & A. He lived in Devon. His landscapes were characterised by tranquility and a subtle transfusion of atmosphere.

He was an outstanding painter of farm-horses.

Coll: V. & A., Exeter A.G.

BAKER, ARTHUR. op. 1864-1911

This minor painter of his period produced sporting and animal compositions in both oil and watercolours. He lived in London and at Tunbridge Wells. He painted in Essex, Northern France, and Scotland in 1885 and 1889. He was a friend of Alfred Strutt, another painter who included animals in his range. In 1897 Baker painted the Duke of Hamilton's 'Hounds in Kennel' in which each hound depicted is a portrait.

He exhibited 2 works at R.A., 3 at B.I., and 2 at S.S.

BAKER, W. C. 1815-1891

The son of an innkeeper, born at Litcham, Norfolk, he appears to have been self-taught. In this most rural of English counties he gained a local reputation for his portraits of prize-cattle, sheep, horses, and dogs. He possessed talent but lacked the opportunity to make it widely recognised and died in poverty. His portrait of a cob 'Confidence' was engraved in Vol. 133 of the Sporting Magazine and a picture of the West Norfolk Hounds is recorded.

BALDOCK, JAMES WALSHAM.   op 1858-1887
This painter, who worked in both watercolours and oils, lived at Worksop. He painted hunting scenes and competent portraits of horses and cattle in a highly finished manner.
He exhibited 16 works at B.I. and 6 at N.W.C.S.
Illustration in B.S.P.

BALFOUR-BROWNE, VINCENT R.   1880-1963
A pupil of George Lodge, he lived in Dumfrieshire. Working mostly in watercolour his subjects were usually Highland stalking scenes. He illustrated several books and many articles about red deer and made a number of prints from stalking incidents.

*BAMBER, BESSIE.
This Liverpool lady specialised in the painting of domestic cats and kittens.

BARBER, CHARLES BURTON.   1845-1894
Born in Great Yarmouth and after studying in the R.A. Schools, he worked in both oils and watercolours. His subjects were sporting scenes and animals. Patronised by Queen Victoria, he painted the Spanish Oxen at Osborne pulling a hay-cart, a Wild Boar and Sow with their litter, and the Queen's fox-terrier 'Flo' with her puppies.
His R.A. exhibits included portraits of the Emperor Napoleon's Charger and the Prince of Wales' Siberian Dog.
His unfamiliar work has yet to re-appear frequently before the common gaze.
Coll: The Royal Coll.
He exhibited 32 works at R.A. from 1866 and 2 at S.S.

BARENGER, JAMES, Jnr.   1780-c.1831
He was the son of James, Snr., a painter of insects, and a nephew of W. Woollett, the engraver, whose art he himself never practised. He was versatile in his range of subjects, painting racehorses, deer, and dogs, as well as sporting scenes, in more artistic settings than is usual. Shaw Sparrow found an echo of Wootton in his work, a 'certain courtliness with refined stiffness' but did not put him in the same class as the old Master. A sportsman himself who bred pointers, the details in his sporting pictures were always accurate. His first exhibits at the R.A. in 1807 were 'Sheep from Nature' and 'A Famous Setter'.
His 'Lord Derby's Staghounds' of 1819 in the Mellon Coll. is considered the best of his hunting scenes.
He exhibited 48 works at the R.A., and 8 at the B.I.
Coll: Walker A.G.
Illustration in B.S.P.

BARKER, Benjamin, Snr.   c. 1739-1793
The fame of this Barker rests on being the sire of the 'Barkers of Bath' rather than on his scanty merits as an animal painter. Born at Newark-on-Trent, he started his working life as a decorator of japaned ware, but changed horses and became the owner of a livery stable. The outcome of these successive careers was that he took up his brushes again to paint portraits of horses. These are said to be inferior.
Although his talented children frequently included cattle and other animals in their work, they rate as landscapists and pastoralists rather than animal painters.

BARKER, JOHN JOSEPH.   op. 1835-1863
One of the Barker family of Bath, he made pen and wash drawings of animals and figures.
It is thought that he was not the same John Barker who painted sheep with sheep-dogs in Highland scenery in a highly finished manner.

BARKER, WRIGHT.   op. 1884-?1935
He painted hunting scenes, horses, and Highland cattle, and more occasionally, landscape.
His picture of some Rufford Hunt Hounds in Kennel has affinity with the works of Emms (q.v.) and Noble (q.v.).

12

*BARLOW, FRANCIS.   c.1626-1704

This early English painter of birds, fish, and animals came to London, according to Vertue, from Lincoln-shire and was apprenticed to William Shepherd the court portrait painter. He developed a style based on close observation that had little in common, other than subject matter, with his exotic contemporaries, Bogdani, Hondius, and Knyff.

His earliest known work, dated 1648, is a drawing of 'David Slaying the Lion', now in the British Museum; the following year his engraving of Princess Elizabeth was published in the Hague. In 1650 on completion of his apprenticeship, he was admitted to the freedom of the Company of Painter-Stainers.

In 1652 he made some of the illustrations for the poet Benlowes' 'Theophila' and produced an 'Aesop's Fables' illustrated with 110 of his etchings that ran to 3 editions. Although he was generally known in his day as a painter and denied that he was an etcher by profession, his paintings, often large, passed into private possession and obscurity, while his drawings, much used by Hollar and Fairthorne for engraving, remained in the public eye.

The quality of his paintings and of his smaller work that shows so vividly the rural life of his age, place him far above his contemporaries. Shaw Sparrow called him the Father of Sport in Art.

Coll: The B.M. (52), the Tate, V. & A. (3), the Mellon Coll., the Preston, Bedford, Plymouth and Newcastle A.G's.

BARRATT, THOMAS.   op. from 1852-189 ?

This Stockbridge man painted landscape and animals – horses, deer, dogs, and game.

His 'Sultan', winner of the 1855 Cambridgeshire, was shown at the R.A. in 1856. In following years he showed 'Red Deer in Windsor Park' at the B.I., and 'Deer in Ashstead Park' at the R.A.

He exhibited 17 works at R.A., 6 at B.I., 11 at S.S.

BARRAUD, HENRY.   1811-1874

Younger by a year than his brother, William, they were the sons of a Customs House official. The brothers shared a studio and worked in collaboration, exhibiting sporting scenes and portraits both singly and jointly, and achieving a wide popularity with owners of horses, hounds and dogs. Henry continued to produce such work after his brother's early death and also painted genre of Victorian feeling. His choristers entitled 'We Praise Thee, O God' and the 'London Season', set in Hyde Park, were composed to be engraved, the latter with a key giving the names of the notabilities depicted. His picture of 'Bakewell Leicester Sheep' was engraved by Hanhart. The Old Sporting Magazine published in all only 7 prints from his work.

He exhibited 33 works at R.A. from 1842-1849, 48 works at B.I. from 1840-1849, and 19 at S.S.

BARRAUD, WILLIAM.   1810-1850

More talented than his brother Henry, he was a worthy pupil of his master, Abraham Cooper, and had he not died at 40, might have rivalled Ferneley. He started work as a clerk in the Customs House before devoting himself solely to art, so that his productive years were short. During these he painted occasionally in watercolour. Among the engravings after his works that were published in the Old Sporting Magazine was a portrait of the racehorse 'British Volunteer' and 4 prints of greyhounds. Shaw Sparrow considered that 'he had a genuine talent with a feeling for weight and a manly rhythm of line'.

He exhibited 58 works at R.A. from 1830-1849, and 36 at B.I. from 1835-1849.

Illustration in B.S.P.

Coll: V. & A.

BARRINGTON-BROWNE, W. E.   1908 - living artist

Son of the pastellist, H. Nedeham-Browne, he was educated at Repton and Pembroke College. He studied art in Venice and at Julian's in Paris. For 10 years he was Art Master at Cheltenham.

His subjects are usually stalking and fishing scenes and studies of deer.

He first exhibited in London in 1966 at the Tryon Gallery.

BARWICK, JOHN.   op. 1839-1870

A native of Beverley, Yorks., he lived his working life in Doncaster, where he died. He had skill as a portrait painter of huntsmen and horses and was patronised by Lords Fitzwilliam and Willoughby d'Eresby. He exhibited 2 pictures at the R.A., one being of the latter's horses in 1849. The Sport Magazine of 1839 published plates of his 'Mr. Barber on his hunter Billy' and of 'Dash', a retriever. The Scot, J. W. Giles, made lithographs after some of his pictures of cattle.

BATEMAN, JAMES. 1814-1849

The son of a Billingsgate fish-dealer, he began his working career as a clerk. In art he was self-taught and it was not until after his marriage in 1836 that he gave up clerking for painting. He first exhibited at the B.I. in 1840 and at the R.A. in 1841. The Sporting Magazine published the first of 45 plates from his work in 1840. It is surprising that despite his many pictures of Indian sporting scenes, he never left England : these were composed from descriptions givn by a friend. He became an intimate of Landseer, sharing a studio with him and inevitably absorbing some of his style. He attained great skill in portraying all animals and became especially fond of painting foxes.

His career as an artist only lasted 9 years. He died aged 34 before reaching full recognition.

He exhibited 19 works at R.A., 12 at B.I., and 33 at S.S.

BATEMAN, JAMES, R.A. 1893-1959

He studied at the Royal College of Art and at the Slade. While employed as an art master he made himself into a painter and engraver of distinction. Many of his subjects were pastoral.

His 'Mare and Foal' is in the Leeds A.G. His 'Elephant and Castle Horse Fair' was exhibited in 1949 at the R.A.

Coll : The Tate, B.M., Vancouver, Adelaide, Sydney, Leeds, Newcastle and Southampton A.G's.

BATT, J. ARTHUR. op. 1875-1897

He painted, in an uninspiring manner, small pictures, sometimes on panel, of domestic animals and birds. Like William Weekes he had a partiality for donkeys, occasionally setting them in landscapes of large size. He lived at Romsey.

He exhibited 4 works at R.A., and 14 at S.S.

BEATTIE, LUCAS. op. 1830's

Nothing has yet come to light about this artist. His rare work includes the portrait of the racehorse 'Elis', with jockey up, in a racecourse setting, and 'A Mare and Foal' in a landscape dated 1834, which displays more than average talent.

BEAVIS, RICHARD, R.W.S. 1824-1896

Born at Exmouth, he studied at the R.A. Schools before gaining employment as an artist and designer with the firm of Trollope, decorators and upholsterers, with whom he worked until 1863. He spent two years from 1867 at Boulogne when he came under the influence of Millet and the Barbizon school. In 1875 he travelled to Venice and the Near East.

He worked in oils and watercolours over a wide range of subjects which included landscape, Eastern, military, and rustic scenes as well as animals. These latter included portraits of hunters and pictures of deer.

BEER, JOHN. op. 1900's-1910

Working in both oils and watercolour, this painter produced portraits of racehorses and racing scenes and worked as an illustrator.

He painted the Duke of Westminster's 'Flying Fox,' winner of the 1899 Derby. 'Doncaster Horse Sales' and watercolours of the Grand National of 1909 and 1910 are recorded.

Artistically he was small beer.

BELLINGER, —. op. 1803

He sent 3 pictures to the R.A. in this year from Kentish Town. One was of bear-hunting and another of 'A Man with a Spaniel'.

BENINGFIELD, GORDON. Living Artist

He works in watercolours and specialises in depicting the smaller mammals of the English countryside, such as voles and shrews.

He has been exhibiting at the Moorland Gallery in London since 1968.

BENNET, THOMAS. op. 1796-1819 ? 28

This Woodstock artist's seven exhibits sent to the R.A. included portraits of dogs and hunters. The latter are of high quality both in composition and colouring. Charles Turner produced 9 mezzo-tints from 1807-1828 after him, of Hounds, Hares, Badgers, and Foxes, with and without their progeny. Whessel engraved

14

a plate from his 'William Phelp on his Pony with Hounds' in 1812. He exhibited at the O.W.C.S. from 1816-1819.

BENSON, J. op. 1805-1811
This landscape and sporting artist also painted portraits of animals. He exhibited at the R.A. 'Coursing' in 1807, 'Portrait of a Pointer' in 1809, and 'Warrior, a Favourite Hunter' in 1811. Two other exhibits were views in Lancashire, of which, perhaps, he was a native.

BERKELEY, STANLEY R. E. op. 1878-1902 d.1909
Living in Surrey and London, he painted animals, historical, battle, and sporting scenes in oils and water-colours.
His R.A. exhibits ranged from 'Full Cry' to 'For God and the King'.
He exhibited 16 works at R.A., 14 at SS, and 9 at N.W.C.S.

BEST, JOHN. op. 1750-1792
Little is known about this early painter who exhibited 7 works at the S.A. and 3 at the R.A. between 1772-1787. In 1782 he painted 'A Large Ox' for Robert Bakewell, one of the fathers of cattle-breeding in this country; in 1787 he painted 'A Warwickshire Ox', and in 1791 he portrayed the Derby winner of that year, 'Eager'. He copied other painters' works: one that he did of the Waldegrave Family being an excellent copy of Stubbs' picture.
Two plates engraved from his work of 'Gamecocks' appeared in the first volume of the Sporting Magazine in 1792. In his 'An Officer with his Bay Hunter and Dog' in a landscape painted in 1776, his handling of the animals places him in the class of 'semi-primitives'.

BEVAN, ROBERT POLHILL. 1865-1925
Born at Hove, he studied at the Westminster School of Art before going to Julian's in Paris. After visiting North Africa he settled in Hampstead.
He developed a highly individual angular style of his own. His favourite subjects were scenes of horses at sale yards. These are of high artistic quality that place him far above contemporary horse-painters. He was an outstanding lithographer.
He was one of the foundation members of the Campden Town Group in 1911.
Coll: Tate, Leicester A.G.

BEWICK, THOMAS. 1753-1828
The son of a Northumbrian farmer, he was born at Eltringham. His talent for drawing from Nature became apparent before he was apprenticed to a Newcastle engraver, Ralph Beilby, with whom he became skilled in wood-cutting. After a few months in London in 1776, he returned to enter into partnership with his former master who wrote the text to his 'General History of Quadrupeds', published in 1790. This brought him recognition. In 1789 he produced his block of the 'Chillingham Bull' which he considered his most successful individual commission. His most famous work, 'The History of British Birds', was published in 2 vols. in 1797 and 1804, the engravings being superior to those of the 'Quadrupeds'.
In his leisure from his engraving business, he produced delicate watercolours of Birds and Vignette engravings of rural scenes, often incorporating rustic humour, that he called his 'tale-pieces'. His 'Aesop's Fables' published in 1818 were not a success, after a severe illness had necessitated the engravings being cut by his pupils from his designs. In his last 6 years he was engaged in an unillustrated 'Memoir' in which he describes his engraving technique of slightly lowering that part of the block which was the background to his design, so as to emphasise the central figures. He was the first to develop this method successfully and few of his many followers used it with such charming results.
The ornithologist William Yarrell named Bewick's Swan in his honour.
Coll: The V. & A. (2), the B.M. (230), and at Newcastle.

BIEGEL, PETER. 1913 - living artist
Educated at Downside, he was a pupil of Lucy Kemp-Welsh at Bushey. After war service he studied at Bournemouth and under Lionel Edwards and developed a not dissimilar style. He has painted many racing, hunting and sporting pictures in Britain and the U.S.A. A racing and hunting man, he knows his subjects thoroughly and successfully transmits the atmosphere of the incidents that he portrays. He lives in Dorset.

BINKS, REUBEN WARD.
This painter of sporting scenes in oils and watercolours specialised in portraying gun-dogs.
He illustrated Croxton-Smith's 'About our Dogs' and Patrick Chambers' 'Gun Dogs'. He went to live in New York.

BIRD, HARRINGTON. op. 1870-1899
This Victorian painted sporting subjects and portraits of animals. Among those of racehorses was that of 'Persimmon' who won the Derby of 1896 and was owned by the Prince of Wales.

*BLINKS, THOMAS. 1860-1912
He produced work of almost photographic exactitude while still infusing is his compositions a certain flavour of Victorian sentimentality, whether of hounds marking their fox to ground or of setters working on the moors. His detailed pictures of gun-dogs of this breed are so highly finished that he might well be dubbed the 'Master of the Immaculate Setter'.
Some of his work of the 1880's was engraved by J. B. Pratt.
He exhibited at R.A. from 1886-1904 and at S.S. (4).
Coll: Leicester A.G.
Illustration in B.S.P.

BOGDANI, JAKOB. -1724
A Hungarian who came to this country in the reign of Queen Anne, it is recorded that he had no formal training in art. His decorative work, consisting of paintings of indigenous and exotic birds, faithfully copied from Nature, was usually placed over fireplaces and doorways.
Queen Anne bought from Admiral Churchill's executors a set of Bogdani's paintings done for his Aviary at Ranger's Lodge, Windsor. These are still in the Royal Collection. Included in them are chital, gazelle, and antelope; it was his wont to include other smaller mammals in his large pictures of birds.
Coll: The Fitzwilliam and Nottingham A.G.

BOTTOMLEY, JOHN WILLIAM. 1816-1900.
After studying in Munich and Dusseldorf, he settled in London where he became an animal and sporting painter of repute, occasionally painting pure landscape. The scenery in his compositions was of a high standard.
He was another artist who inserted the cattle in Creswick's landscapes. His R.A. exhibits included a 'Fox in Cover', 'Deer Stalking', and a 'Change of Dogs'.
He exhibited 37 pictures at R.A., 16 at B.I., 3 at S.S.

BOULT, A. S. op. 1815-1853
Facts about this sporting artist are scarce save that he started his working life in the Stag Brewery in London. He achieved a considerable degree of competence in both oil and watercolour, painting sporting scenes and some portraits of horses.
He contributed 10 works to the R.A., 4 to B.I., and 3 to S.S,
llustration in B.S.P.

BOULTBEE, JOHN. 1742-1812
This Leicestershire-born painter was much influenced by Stubbs, though there is no record of his having been his pupil, and his talents were greatly inferior. Mostly he painted horses and a few portraits of cattle that were engraved. In contrast to the firm handling of his horses, his pure landscapes were done in a somewhat pale and indeterminate style. His 'Durham Ox' was engraved by Whessel.
He exhibited 6 works at R.A., 3 at S.A., 3 at F.S., of which 6 were landscapes.
Coll: York and Leicester A.G's.
Illustration in B.S.P.

BOULTBEE, THOMAS. op. 1775-1783
The brother of John, with whom he lived in London, their work is hard to distinguish. He too exhibited 12 pictures there and he too painted for T. W. Coke at Loughborough, exhibiting his 'Hunter and Shooting Horse' at R.A. in 1783.

BRANSCOMBE, CHARLES.   op. 1805-1809
This animal painter produced portraits of race-horses and dogs in a style that shows more than primitive talent and recalls that of Edwin Cooper. It can be assumed that he was provincial as he did not exhibit in London. A portrait of 'Ajax', a celebrated pointer, in an extensive landscape containing a horseman and other dogs, is recorded. He is known to have worked in Nottingham.

*BREACH, E. E.   op. 1868-1886
This Victorian's 'forte' was painting gun-dogs on the moors. In 1875 his exhibit at the R.A. was entiled 'A brace : steady at the point'.
Another picture dated 1876 was of 'Floss and Bloom', two pointers, in a Highland setting. He produced compositions of puppies and kittens in the manner of Couldery.
He exhibited 1 work at R.A. and 33 at S.S.

BRETLAND, THOMAS W.   1802-1874
Born and dying in Nottingham, after a start in commerce he became a well-known local painter of race-horses and animals, and was patronised by the Dukes of Buccleugh and Montrose. He was fond of painting, as backgrounds to his portraits, the Georgian houses of his subjects' owners. He did not exhibit during his lifetime and his work passing directly into private collections, it is only recently that his art has become more widely recognised.
He must be regarded as a provincial horse-painter of the 1st class. His best-known work is of Major Burton at Balaclava.
Coll : The Nottingham and York City A.G's.

BRISTOW, EDMUND.   1787-1876
This 'Little Master' of English landscape painting cannot be ommitted from this volume. Living his long life at Windsor, which so often figures in his small equisite landscape work, he produced many pictures of dogs, donkeys , and horses, often in humorous compositions, as well as portraits and sporting scenes; some of these were engraved.
He exhibited 12 works at R.A., 11 at B.I., and 8 at S.S.
Coll : Hull and Leicester A.G's.
Illustration in B.S.P.

BRITTAN, CHARLES E, Snr.   op. 1860-1890
This Plymouth man, working only in the West Country, painted animals and birds in oils and watercolour. Portraits of a race-horse and of dogs are recorded as well as studies of a Tiger, a Golden Eagle, and King-fishers.
His son, also C. E. Brittan, was a landscape artist.
Coll : Plymouth A.G.

BROOKE, WILLIAM.   op. 1779-1783
This early cattle painter exhibited at the R.A. during these years.

*BROWNE, E.   op. 1838-1857
He worked in Coventry and Warwickshire painting horses, dogs, the occasional cavalry scene, and chargers. His picture dated 1840 of 'Three Gun Dogs' by a shed with a country house in the background is well composed and competently painted. A portrait of the horse 'Stockwell' dated 1853, with attendant terriers in a stable-yard displays more merit than the work of many of his better-known contemporaries. A Horse and Dog portrait of 1848 showed Bulkington Church in the background : he painted some pictures for the Warners of that village.

BROWN, Sir JOHN ALFRED ARNESBY, R.A.   1866-1955
Born in Nottingham, he studied at that city's School of Art before going to the Herkomer School at Bushey. He became a landscapist of great distinction, carrying on the tradition of Constable in East Anglia where he painted in oils and watercolours.
His treatment of the cattle and sheep in his compositions raised him artistically far above the usual run of animal painters.

Three of his works were purchased by the Chantrey Bequest and are in the Tate.
Coll: Tate, Liverpool, Nottingham, Preston and Cape Town A.G's.

BROWN, NATHANIEL.   op. 1753-1779
This versatile 18th century artist covered a wide range of subjects including portraits, classical, historical, and sea-pieces – in all, exhibiting 54 works at the F.S.
His portrait of a 'Gentleman standing by his Hunter with Hounds in a Landscape' is happier in its composition and setting than in the portrayal of the animals.
Illustration in B.S.P.

BROWN, R. G.   op. 1844
Work by this Victorian is rare but common. His 'Three Hunters at a Paddock Gate' does not display more than moderate ability in depicting either them or the landscape.
A grey pony with a spaniel in a stable and Two Pointers at Work are also recorded.

BULLEY, ASHBURNHAM H.   op. 1841-1861
The three pictures that this man sent from a London address to the R.A. were of a Vixen and of dogs.
He exhibited 3 works at R.A., 13 at B.I., 7 at S.S.

BURBANK, J. M.   op. 1825-d.1873
This Camberwell man painted animals and birds in oils and watercolours. He is known to have travelled in America.
He started exhibiting at R.A. in 1825, showing 'A Dog's Head'. His 1845 exhibit there was 'A Giraffe Attacked by a Lion'.
He sent 12 works to R.A., 6 to B.I., 19 to S.S., and 21 to N.W.C.S.

BURNET, JAMES M.   1788-1816
This Scotsman is said to have been born in Musselburgh. He made a reputation as a painter of cattle before leaving Edinburgh in 1810 to join his brother John in London. Taking Paul Potter as his Master his work suggests talent that his short life precluded from flowering. His subjects were pastoral scenes in which cattle predominated. His brother engraved some of his work to illustrate his book on landscape painting published in 1849.
He exhibited 9 works at R.A. and 23 at B.I.

BUTLER, Lady, née ELIZABETH SOUTHERDEN THOMPSON.   1850-1933
Born in Lausanne, this gifted woman painter, a sister of Alice Meynell the poetess, produced equestrian and military pictures. Her 'Rollcall', at the R.A. in 1874, was bought by Queen Victoria. She exhibited 'Inkermann' there in 1877, the year in which she married Major, later General Sir William Butler.
Through its many reproductions her 'Remnant of an Army', showing the exhausted Dr. Brydon reeling in his saddle on his arrival at Jellabad, the sole survivor of the Army from Kabul, stirred the Empire as much as her well-known 'Scotland for Ever'.

BUTLER, THOMAS.   op. 1750-1759
A book-seller and stationer of Pall Mall, in 1750 he issued a circular stating that he and his assistants were ready to visit patrons' seats to paint their horses, dogs, hunts, etc.
There is some doubt that he himself actually painted many of these pictures. A version of Morier's standard portrait of the Godolphin Arabian inscribed by him is in the Royal Collection and 2 other portraits of 'Brisk – a Hunter' and 'A Hunter' dated 1759 are also inscribed. Many others are inscribed as painted *at* Thos. Butler's, Pall Mall.
Perhaps his importance lay in the employment that he gave his assistants: it is regretted that they remained un-named, though it is believed that one of them was Thomas Spencer (*q.v.*).

BYNG, ROBERT.   op. 1704-d.1723
There is doubt about the identity of this fine artist whose claim to inclusion here rests on one large canvas dated 1706 but signed without an initial. Although the central figure was unfinished, this beautifuly painted picture of hounds and huntsmen in a landscape can only arouse regret that more of his work of this nature is not known.

18

His portraits of Joseph Pullen, General Charles Montagu, Sir Michael Earle, and a plate engraved from his 'Underhill as Obadiah' in 'The Fantastic Elder' are conventional work of that period. He is said to have worked in the studio of Kneller who died in 1702. One of his early works is the group portrait of the Sutton children with a pet deer in an interior, dated 1704.

In 1782 C. R. Riley engraved his 'Deer Hunt'.

Illustration in B.S.P.

CALDECOTT, RANDOLPH, R. I.   1846-1886

Son of a Chester accountant, his natural gift for drawing beasts and birds continued to develop while he was employed as a bank clerk in Manchester. In 1872 he went to London and received commissions for drawings in several periodicals while working in the studio of Dalon, the sculptor, and at the Slade.

He illustrated Washington Irvine's 'Sketch-book' that appeared in 1875. This was followed by other successful productions which made his name as an illustrator of popular children's books. A bronze bas relief, 'Horse Fair in Brittany' was considered the best example of his modelling. His drawings of horses and dogs were made with the intimate knowledge of a sportsman while his compositions reflected his kind and humorous disposition.

Coll: The Tate, V. & A., Manchester, Bristol and Newport A.G's.

*CALDERON, WILLIAM FRANK, R.O.I.   1865-1943

The son of Philip, R.A., he studied at the Slade under Le Gros. He painted landscape, portraits, and sporting scenes. In 1894 he founded the School of Animal Painting where Munnings, Lionel Edwards, and Cecil Aldin were pupils. An outstanding draughtsman and sketcher, he was less happy with his larger canvasses.

His 'Horse Fair' exhibited at the R.A. in 1894, was considered one of his best works. He published 'Animal Painting and Anatomy' in 1936.

He exhibited 19 works at R.A., 3 at S.S. from 1881.

CALVERT, HENRY.   op. 1813-1861

This fine Manchester artist produced robust work of quality, painting many portraits of horses and dogs as well as several set pieces of hunts. His 'Vine Hunt Meeting' was engraved by W. H. Simmons in 1844. His 'Wynstay Hunt' shown at the R.A. in 1852 was engraved by W. T. Davey in 1855. His last picture to be exhibited at the R.A. in 1854 was of Cheetahs.

His work outshines that of many of his contemporaries.

He exhibited 4 works at R.A. from 1826-1854.

Illustration in B.S.P.

CANTELO, C.   op. 1863-1864

A crude portrait of 'Queen Bertha', winner of the Oaks of 1863, was made by this man. Her owner, Lord Falmouth, had the only bet (of 6d.) of his life on this horse: he presented his stake set in a cluster of diamonds to the fair winner of the wager.

A set of 4 small hunting scenes by Cantelo dated 1864 is also recorded.

CARTER, HENRY N.   op. 1860-1894

Little is known about this minor animal painter. 'Waiting for Master' is recorded as an example of his work. He did not exhibit in London.

CARTER, SAMUEL JOHN.   1835-1892

This Norfolk-born artist rises above the ruck of many Victorian horse-painters despite his frequent employment in turning out the likenesses of favourite hunters in the stereotyped manner of the day. He painted horses with accuracy and feeling and could display a good sense of composition, producing some excellent equestrian portraits in pleasing settings.

His exhibits at the R.A. between 1855-90 included sporting scenes of stag-hunting. He was particularly successful in painting red deer, one of these subjects being acquired by the Tate Gallery. A presentation picture 'A September Evening, Badgworthy', was a skilful composition in which he painted both a horse and a stag. Shaw Sparrow considered that his sporting work marked a phase in the transition towards the modern outlook of benevolence to animals.

He exhibited at R.A. (49), at B.I. (3), and at S.S. (10).

Coll: The Tate, Preston.

CATTON, CHARLES, R.A. 1728-1798

A native of Norwich, he first received attention as a painter of heraldry and hatchments and became coach-painter to Geo. III. Advancing from painting coaches to painting horses, he went on to produce subjects from the Classics and History as well as painting animals and landscape, often on a large scale. His animal subjects included lions, tigers, dogs, horses, and cattle. He was elected a foundation member of the R.A., where he exhibited in all 43 works as well as 16 at S.A.

CATTON, CHARLES, Jnr. 1756-1819

Following his father in the lucrative profession of coach-painting he also produced well-painted animals and landscape in both oil and watercolours. He made illustrations for several magazines and engraved some prints after Morland.

Among the 37 exhibits sent to the R.A. between 1776 and 1800 was 'A Horse Race' in 1786 which was successful enough to be engraved. In 1804 he emigrated to America where he died.

Coll: V. & A.

CERVENG, JOHN. op. 1771-1773

This painter of portraits and animals is recorded as having exhibited 5 works at S.A., and 2 at R.A. They included pictures of a dog, of a horse, and of a leopard, and 2 equestrian military portraits.

CHALON, FRANCIS. 1776-1836

'A sporting painter of repute' – Grant.

CHALON, HENRY BERNARD. 1771-1849

Son of a Dutch music-teacher and his runaway well-bred English wife, he studied at the R.A. Schools and was exhibiting at the age of 22. He was made Animal Painter to the Duchess of York in 1795 and, later on, to the Prince Regent and William IV. He married, like Morland, one of the James Ward's sisters, and, like Garrard, reached maturity early. Painting in a good solid style he seems to have been detached from his contemporaries and was lucky to be well-patronised during the depression of the Napoleonic wars when artists such as Reinagle were in distress. He was well-served by such able mezzotinters as William Ward and Charles Turner. He often painted on a large scale, his animals being anatomically correct, though the tone of his pictures could be dull. He painted portraits of horses, dogs and cattle. His best picture is thought to be 'The Prince Regent's Staghounds Unkennelling at Ascot Heath' in which all the figures are portraits – painted in 1817.

In 1837 he published 'Passions of the Horse' illustrated by lithographs expressing this animal's emotions.

He was not related to the brothers A. E. and J. J. Chalon, R.A's.

He exhibited 198 works at R.A., 28 at B.I., 22 at S.S.

Illustration in B.S.P.

Coll: Diploma Gal. R.A., V. & A., Mellon Coll., & Walker A.G.

CHARLTON, JOHN, R.B.A. 1849-1917

This Northumbrian painter was a student at the Newcastle School of Art and later at South Kensington.

Shaw Sparrow considered him a connecting link between his predecessors and the more modern school of animal painters headed by Munnings. Starting his career by painting portraits of horses, he progressed, unaffected by current trends in art, to sporting and equestrian groups, to battle-scenes, and to State occasions – all painted in a smooth lush style that became more mannered as time went on.

As an animal painter, however, he remains pre-eminent in portraying foxhounds; of all our animal painters he has few equals in 'getting' a hound's character. With his horses he was not so outstanding. He made the illustrations of deer and hounds in the Badminton Library volume on hunting.

He exhibited 37 works at R.A. and 21 at S.S.

CHRISTMAS, THOMAS C. op. 1819-1825

His subjects included dogs, cats, horses, and lions. One of his R.A. exhibits that were sent from a London address was a portrait of a horse.

He exhibited 2 works at R.A., 11 at B.I., 6 at S.S., and 5 at O.W.C.S.

CLARK, ALBERT JAMES, Snr. op. *c.* 1890-*c.*1909

This sound craftsman was employed in taking likenesses in paint of people's hunters and racehorses which he did well enough – no Herring was he. The occasional prize heifer came his way. He was a capital fellow to paint your carriage-horses, to hang in the servants' hall.

He painted the portraits of 'Ballentrae', winner of the 1897 Cambridgeshire, 'Copper King', and 'Pretty Polly'.

CLARK, FREDERICK ALBERT. op. 1906-1909

He painted the portraits of several celebrated trotting horses such as 'School Girl' and 'Dublin Daisy', as well as many hunters.

He is believed to have been a son of Albert James Clark.

He did not exhibit in London.

CLARK, JAMES. op. c. 1892-1899

This son of Albert came from the same stable, holding paint not dandy brushes: his subjects were the same as Father's; hunters, coach-horses, and the rarer race-horse. Sometimes he let his fancy free and painted a 'loose horse' following a hunt or a runaway coach-horse. He painted the famous 'Flying Fox' winner of the 1899 Derby, 2,000 Guineas, and St. Leger.

Coll: Reading.

CLAUSEN, Sir GEORGE, R.A. 1852-1944

A Londoner, the son of a Danish sculptor, he studied at the South Kensington Schools and in Paris under Bouguereau and Robert-Fleury. He was influenced by Millet and, later, by the Impressionists.

He worked in oils and watercolours. His output included portraits but was mainly landscape and agricultural compositions. His mastery of conveying the light and atmosphere of his rural scenes and his sympathetic handling of the animals, made him an outstanding pastoralist.

He was a founder member of the N.E.A.C.; was Professor of Painting at the R.A. Schools 1904-1906; became full R.A. in 1908; and was knighted in 1927.

He published 'Six Lectures on Painting' and 'Aims and Ideals in Art'.

*CLEMINSON, ROBERT. op. 1865-1901

A painter of landscape and of Highland game, both dead and alive, and of sporting dogs, his careful work now appears to suffer the defects of his age: there is no record of his having been Landseer's valet.

He exhibited 10 works at B.I. and 5 at S.S.

CLENNELL, LUKE. 1781-1840

This son of a Northumbrian farmer was apprenticed to Thomas Bewick, the wood-engraver, from 1797 to 1804.   He then went to London and was employed making illustrations for topographical works. About 1810 he started working in oils and watercolours and is recorded as having collaborated with Ben Marshall. His range was wide and he cannot strictly be regarded as an animal painter, though his work included 'The Jovial Fox-Hunter', mezzotinted by Lupton, and the dramatic 'Baggage Waggons in a Storm'.

He died insane.

Coll: the V.& A., and Nottingham A.G.

He exhibited 6 works at R.A., 15 at B.I., and 18 at O.W.C.S.

CLIFTON, F. op. 1790's

A few horse portraits by this artist are recorded. One is of a bay horse named 'York Minster' standing in a loose-box, s. & d. 179-; another is of a Mare and Foal outside a stable.

CLOWES, DANIEL. c. 1790-1849

He was a sporting painter whose portraits of hunters and race-horses are of somewhat wooden appearance. His human figures and backgrounds in these pictures do not exhibit great artistic talent though the subjects were said to be faithful likenesses.

He painted 'Touchstone', the winner of the 1834 St. Leger, several times. He considered his best work to be his 'Ferry House and Boat at Eccleston' but his landscape work is not widely known. His 'Hackney and Springer' was engraved in 1824.

He never exhibited in London.

His son Fred was a more indifferent painter of animals. It was said that their own opinion of their talents was so much higher than generally accepted that they made only a precarious living in exercising them.

COLE, GEORGE.   1810-1883
Born at Portsmouth, he was a self-taught artist who started his career painting animals there. It was not until his return from Holland, where he went to study the Dutch Masters, that he started to exhibit in London, from 1840, portraits and landscape as well as animals.
He became a popular and prolific landscapist but was inferior to his son, George Vicat Cole, R.A.
Coll: Southampton, Bournemouth.
He exhibited 16 works at R.A., 35 at B.I., 209 at S.S.
Illustration in B.S.P.

COLLINS, CHARLES.   1680-1744
An important early painter of birds and animals of the time of Barlow and Cradock, little is known about his life. His style had the precision of a miniaturist. He was adept at catching the characteristic pose of a bird.
In 1736 Fletcher and Mynde engraved a set of 12 plates of 100 British birds made from his drawings.
Coll: Nat. Gal. of Ireland, the Royal Coll., and Bedford A.G.

COLLINS, CHARLES J.   op. 1867-?1903
This modest painter of landscape, in which animals figure predominantly, should not of course be confused with his earlier and more illustrious namesake.
It is thought that he lived in Dorking: he did some work in Devon.

COLMORE, NINA, M.B.E.   1889 - living artist
After studying at Heatherley's and at Julian's in Paris, she became a successful painter of equestrian portraits, race-horses, and hounds, receiving commissions from Royalty, Maharajahs, and many M.F.H's.
Much of her work remains still in private ownership.
Illustration in B.S.P.

COOPER, ABRAHAM, R.A.   1787-1868
He was first employed by his uncle, the manager of Astley's Circus, where his natural talent for drawing animals had full scope. When he was 22 his uncle recognised his determination to be a professional animal painter and introduced him to Ben Marshall, who, impressed by his gifts and industry, took him into his studio and gave him free instruction. Within 2 years the Old Sporting Magazine published the first of 189 plates from his work. He quickly made his reputation as a painter of dogs and horses.
He became an A.R.A. in 1817 and full R.A. in 1820, and continued to exhibit at R.A. for the rest of his life. He was in fashionable demand to paint the winners of the Classic races and always placed his subjects in well-painted landscape settings. His beautifully painted portrait of 'Adonis', Geo. III's favourite Arab charger, compares strikingly with James Ward's dramatic rendering of the same subject.
Cooper's later attempts at wider fields than horse portraiture were extremely popular: his battle-scenes of Marston Moor and other bygone conflicts in which horses predominated, were greeted with acclaim and he was called the English Horace Vernet.
Herring Senior and Wm. Barraud were among his pupils.
He must be admitted to the first rank of animal painters of his age.
He exhibited 332 works at R.A., 74 at B.I., 1 at S.S., 13 at O.W.C.S.
Illustration in B.S.P.

COOPER, ALEXANDER DAVIS.   op. 1837-1888
The son of Abraham Cooper, he followed his father's profession, painting landscape, portraits, and sporting subjects, including animals, but profession it remained– there was no genius there.
He exhibited 67 works at the R.A. – 11 of which were of animals or sporting subjects, the rest landscape, 27 at the B.I., and 16 at S.S.

COOPER, EDWIN.   1785-1833   'of Beccles'
This sterling painter of animals and sporting scenes became known as Cooper of Beccles to distinguish him from the many other artists of that surname. He was the son of Daniel Cooper, drawing-master at Bury School.
His early work was mostly of coaching scenes, some of which were shown at the Ackerman Gallery. He worked at Norwich, Cambridge, and Newmarket.

He painted many portraits of horses, hounds, and dogs, executed in a strong and virile manner and displaying a commanding knowledge of anatomy : his animals are beautifully 'muscled up'. His sporting scenes show that he knew his subject thoroughly.

Coll : V. & A. (1 drawing), Norwich A.G.

He exhibited 2 works at R.A.

Illustration in B.S.P.

COOPER, THOMAS GEORGE. 1835-1901

This Cooper's claim to notice is because he was sired by Thomas Sydney Cooper and followed him as a painter of animals, landscape, and rustic scenes, exhibiting his work at the R.A. and B.I. between 1861-1896. It may be suspected that many a 'Sydney Cooper' was sired by Thomas George.

He exhibited 32 works at R.A., 3 at B.I.

*COOPER, THOMAS SYDNEY, R.A. 1803-1902

Born in Canterbury and reared in poverty, at 12 he was apprenticed to a coach-painter.

Encouraged by Cattermole and by Doyle, a scene-painter, with whom he worked after leaving the coach-painter, in 1823 he went to London. On Abraham Cooper's recommendation (tho' no relation) he entered the R.A. Schools, but lack of funds forced his return to Canterbury, where he worked for 3 or 4 years as a drawing-master. In 1827 he crossed the Channel and worked his way to Brussels where he became friends with Verboekhaven. Both were greatly influenced by Cuyp and Potter. Cooper took up lithography and painting in oils, his subjects almost entirely cattle in pleasing landscapes, his special line which he pursued successfully for the rest of his long career. He seldom attempted to paint animals in action or to paint portraits of animals.

Two years after returning to London, he started exhibiting in 1833. He was elected A.R.A. in 1845, and between 1848 and 1856 often painted the cattle in the landscapes of F. R. Lee and of Creswick. His middle period between 1848-1860 produced his best work : after 1870 as a result of popularity and affluence, his work tended to become more facile and 'slick'.

He became a full R.A. in 1867.

He exhibited 266 works at R.A., 48 at B.I.

There is hardly a public gallery in Britain that does not possess an example of his work.

CORBET, E. op. 1850-1876

He painted portraits of hunters. An early work of 1850 was of a Huntsman and hounds. He drew many pictures of cattle, sheep and pigs for the Farmers' Magazine.

CORBOULD, ALFRED. op. 1831-1875

An animal and sporting painter, who studied horses at Tattersall's, he painted dogs, shooting scenes, and some landscape.

He started exhibiting at R.A. in 1835.

He exhibited 22 works at R.A., 21 at B.I., 16 at S.S.

CORBOULD, ALFRED HITCHENS. op. 1844-1863

A relation of Alfred C. he likewise painted horses and dogs, including 'Caspar' and 'Duck' belonging to the Prince of Wales.

He exhibited 20 works at R.A. and 18 at B.I.

CORBOULD, ASTER R. C. op. 1842-1877

A brother of Alfred Hitchens C., he painted portraits, equestrian groups, horses, cattle and rural genre. One of his R.A. exhibits was a presentation picture of the Madras Hunt.

His last exhibit, in 1874, at the R.A., where he had been showing since 1850, was his 'Mazeppa'. Sometimes he collaborated with his brother.

He exhibited 35 works at R.A., 32 at B.I., 48 at S.S.

CORDREY, JOHN. op. 1765-1825

This painter specialised in coaching scenes, only occasionally producing pictures of hunting and horses. The former were painted in such detail as to suggest that he started his career painting coaches themselves – while the stylised stiffness of his horses indicate a self-taught artist, whose work, nevertheless, has a 'primitive' appeal. He was fond of dating a picture on the milestone painted in the corner of his composition.

CORNISH, JOHN.   18th century

The work of this early 18th century artist is not so rare as facts about his life. Shaw Sparrow records a long narrow picture of racing at Newmarket which he considered might be an apprentice copy after Tillemans (d. 1723). A portrait of a huntsman mounted on a grey horse in an extensive landscape passed more recently through the sale-rooms.

He may have been the same Cornish who worked in Oxford, painting the portraits of Dr. Haynes, the musician: of Dr. Grainger, the print collector (now in the Nat. Port. Gal.); and of Dr. Charles Rose, of which a print was made.

Two portraits are recorded of young women that show affinity to Knapton, Highmore, and Hayman.

The handling of the horses in other equestrian portraits seen suggest that as an animal artist he must be classified as a 'primitive'.

COTTRELL, H. S.   op. 1840-1860

Little is known about this provincial painter who was employed in painting portraits of hunters and race-horses. He was fond of showing these saddled and usually included a dog in his compositions. He painted hunting scenes.

He did not exhibit in London.

*COULDERY, HORATIO H.   1832-1893

One of a family of Lewisham artists, he was a student at 25 at the R.A. Schools and started exhibiting there in 1864. He specialised in the painting of kittens, producing such works as 'A Game of Hide and Seek' and 'The First Meeting' (with a puppy) which was exhibited at the Graphic Exhibition of Animal Paintings of 1882.

He sent 20 works to the R.A., 13 to the B.I. and 62 to S.S.

Coll: Norwich and Nottingham A.G's.

CRADOCK, MARMADUKE   c. 1660-1717

Born at Somerton, Somerset, he came to London and served his apprenticeship to a house-painter. A follower, if not a pupil, of Francis Barlow – his senior by 34 years – in due course his genius, says Vertue, 'distinguished him for one of the best painters of birds and beasts of all his contemporaries. He acquired a very masterly manner, his composition being natural and free, a ready imitation of nature in a broad style of pencilling and force of colouring'.

He painted mainly for dealers, preferring his independance of choice of subject to set commissions. These subjects were mostly of birds, especially of wildfowl, and were painted in a coarser, more strongly-coloured manner than those of Barlow.

CRAWFORD, SUSAN.   1941 -living artist

This artist is the daughter of a racehorse trainer of Haddington Scotland. She studied in Florence under Simi. She paints portraits and dogs, horses, and cattle, and exhibits in London. Her race-horse subjects have included Nijinsky and Sir Ivor. Her reputation deservedly grows as her talents come to full flower.

She first exhibited in London in 1969 at the Tryon Gallery.

*CRAWHALL, JOSEPH.   1861-1913

Born near Morpeth, the son of no ordinary Northumbrian Squire, this talented artist was taught by his father, a close friend of Charles Keene of 'Punch', to draw from memory.

After schooling in London, he studied art for a short time under Morot in Paris before joining the Glasgow Group whose aims were based on broad treatment, sweeping design, and a decorative effect influenced by Japanese and Chinese art. Lavery considered him this Group's most distinguished exponent. He travelled in Spain and Tangiers, being of independant means, and became a perfectionist, ruthlessly destroying work that did not reach his self-imposed standard. A lifelong horseman, he had an intimate knowledge of animals and birds. These were depicted, frequently in gouache on linen, with great simplicity and firmness of line. His work was a real break from the Victorian tradition and places him in the front rank of animal painters of his period. He was a giant among the Balmoral pygmies.

Coll: B.M., Nat. Gal. of Scotland, Burrell Coll. Glasgow, Birmingham and Newcastle A.G's.

CUITT, GEORGE, Snr. 1743-1818

Born at Moulton, Yorkshire, after a sojourn in Italy, he returned to Richmond in the same county where he spent the rest of his life.

He became a popular painter of landscape and country seats, his pictures both in oils and gouache being well composed, though sombre in tone. He was one of the early painters of cattle employed by the pioneer breeders of the Agricultural Revolution to spread the fame of their beasts, their size often being exaggerated.

In 1780 Bailey engraved his portrait of 'The Blakewell Ox', owned by Christopher Hill of Blakewell, Co. Durham, recording beneath the print the animal's detailed vital statistics.

In 1801 Robert Pollard produced a coloured aquatint of his 'Ketton Ox' bred by Charles Colling of Darlington.

He exhibited 14 works at R.A., views of Yorkshire and Wales.

His son, Geo. Jnr., 1779-1854, became an etcher of outstanding merit.

CULLIN, ISAAC J. op. 1883-1920

In addition to painting portraits of famous race-horses, such as 'Zoedone', the 1883 Grand National winner, in which he collaborated with J. A. Wheeler, and 'La Roche', the 1900 Oaks winner, he painted scenes from racing life, such as 'The Saddling Room' at Newmarket with portraits of the jockeys ready to go out, and 'The Paddock' in which the figures of owners, officials, and jockeys are all portraits. Another example was the 'Weighing-in Room, Epsom' shown after the 1883 Derby, from which a print was made.

He did not exhibit in London.

DALBY, DAVID op. 1790-1850 'of York'

Perhaps the son of Dalby, a topographer who drew gentleman's seats and whose works were engraved in Watts' volume in 1780, he was a Yorkshireman who worked in York and Leeds. He became a popular painter of hunters and race-horses, the latter often placed in race-course settings. He usually painted these on small canvasses and in an accurate, highly-finished manner. In 1820 he painted the 'Berkeley Hounds in Kennel' and in 1821 the 'London and Edinburgh Mail Coach', while in 1824 he produced a set of 3 hunting scenes of 'Lord Harewood's Hunt'. His race-horse portraits included 'Blacklock' and 'Velocipede', his son, who won the St. Leger in 1828. Another St. Leger winner, 'St. Patrick', was also painted by him.

Shaw Sparrow records that when he fell on hard times some sportsmen produced 20 hunters whose portraits he painted at 3 gns. each. He was in his prime in the 1820's.

Coll: Walker and York A.G's.

Illustration in B.S.P.

DALBY, JOHN op. 1820's-1850's

There is doubt whether he was a younger brother or son of David D. He also worked in York, painting hunters and race-horses. Much of his work used to be attributed to David, Gilbey and Shaw Sparrow being unaware of his existence.

The small hunting scenes of fine quality that Gilbey admired for their display of the knowledge of hunting and riding and for the anatomical correctness of the drawings were painted by him. Several racing scenes are recorded from his brush.

Coll: Walker and York A.G's.

DANIELL, SAMUEL. *c.* 1775-1811

The nephew of Thomas and younger brother of William Daniell, he had his fair share of the family's artistic talent which was cut short by his early death in Ceylon.

He, too, was a traveller, visiting South Africa and Ceylon and producing volumes with illustrations of scenery, natives, and animals.

The watercolours reproduced in aquatint in his 'African Scenery and Animals' of 1804, include studies of Kudu and impala deer that merit mention in this volume.

Coll: V. & A.

DAVIS, HENRY WILLIAM BANKS, R.A. 1833-1914

The son of a barrister, he studied at the R.A. schools and became a prolific painter of animals and landscape with cattle, etc. Occasionally he produced sculpture.

As a young man he was much influenced by the Pre-Raphaelites but later he produced work, often on large canvasses, that owed more to Landseer. This proved extremely popular.

Two of his pictures were bought by the Chantry Bequest.

He exhibited 100 works at R.A., 5 at B.I., and 17 at S.S.

DAVIS, RICHARD BARRETT, R.B.A.   1782-1854

Born in Watford, the eldest son of Richard Davis, huntsman to the Royal Harriers, and brother of Charles, huntsman of the Royal Buckhounds, he showed early signs of artistic talent. At the insistence of Geo. III Sir Francis Bourgeois took him as a pupil. As early as 1802-3 the R.A. accepted 3 of his landscapes. He continued his training at the R.A. schools and under Sir William Beechey. He became an animal painter of considerable merit, well patronised by Court and Nobility, producing portraits of Mares and Foals, Hunters, Race-horses and of prize cattle. In 1828 he was appointed Animal Painter to the future William IV. Even so he was not elected A.R.A. and thenceforth turned to the Society of British Artists.

When able to escape the conventions of animal portraiture, he could produce landscapes of superior merit. He worked sometimes in watercolours.

He exhibited 70 works at R.A., 57 at B.I., 141 at S.S.

Coll: the Royal Coll., Melton Coll., Hull and Walker A.G's.

Illustration in B.S.P.

DAVIS, WILLIAM HENRY.   op. 1803-d.1865

This artist is recorded as having visited Rome, where he painted landscape, but he was to become well known as a popular sporting and animal painter who received many commissions for portraits of race-horses hunters, and hounds, as well as of prize cattle.

In 1837 he was appointed Animal Painter to William V who died later that year. He was the brother of R. B. Davis who had received this honour 9 years earlier.

He exhibited 30 works at R.A., 7 at B.I., 8 at S.S.

de DREUX, ALFRED.   1810-1860

This French artist, who was born and died in Paris, spent some time in England where his portraits of dogs and horses became popular. His range was wider than this, however, and he excelled in painting women on horseback with an elegance and grace that has seldom been equalled. His equestrian portrait of Queen Victoria riding in Windsor Park with Louis Philippe was lithographed by the artist himself.

Romantic to the end, he was killed in a duel by Comte Fleury, Napoleon III's principal aide-de-camp.

DENEW, RICHARD.   op. 1827-1858

This painter of views in Rome and Venice, which for 30 years he exhibited regularly in London, on occasion painted race-horses. His portraits of 'Stockwell' and of 'Lottery', with Jan Mason up, winner of the Grand National in 1839, are recorded.

He exhibited 6 works at R.A., 1 at B.I., 19 at S.S.

de PRADES, ALFRED F.   op. 1844-1884

He lived in Fitzroy Square, London, though he is known to have worked in Derby. He painted the portraits of race-horses, usually with jockeys mounted, in open landscapes, such as that of 'Dangerous' and of 'Leamington'. J. Moore published his portrait of Nat Langham the jockey in 1853 and a coloured aquatint of the race-horse 'Nancy' was also made.

He painted still life, sporting, and coaching scenes, one of which was a scene outside Aldridge's, Covent Garden, the alternative auction yard to Tattersall's.

His output was not large.

Coll: Bristol A.G.

He exhibited 2 works at R.A., 6 at B.I., 4 at S.S. from 1862-79.

Illustration in B.S.P.

DESVIGNES, EMILY, (Mrs. Bicknell).   op. 1855-1875

The daughter of H. C. Desvignes, she painted cattle and sheep; in fact from the lists of her exhibits she seems to have specialised in sheep-painting to the exclusion of nearly all else.

She exhibited 6 pictures at R.A. and 23 at S.S.

DESVIGNES, HERBERT CLAYTON. op. 1833-1863

This London painter exhibited, over a span of 30 years, pictures of cattle and sheep or of rural scenes in the Home Counties in which they predominate. He also painted hunting and coaching scenes and portraits of horses – that of the race-horse 'Sweetmeat' with jockey and trainer, was engraved by Charles Hunt.
He exhibited 20 pictures at the R.A., 30 at B.I., 34 at S.S.

DICKSEE, HERBERT THOMAS. 1862-?1904

Son of Thomas Francis Dicksee and brother of the future P.R.A., Sir Frank, he painted historical scenes and animals. Lions were his favourite subjects. He exhibited 25 works from 1885-1904 at the R.A. and sent one to S.S.

DIGHTON, JOSHUA. op. 1886-1896

It must be assumed that this painter was of the same family as other minor artists of his name.
He specialised in painting race-horses; these included 'Ilex', winner of the 1890 Grand National, 'Ivor', winner of the 1895 November Handicap, and of 'Old Joe', winner of the 1886 Grand National, painted in watercolour.

DOENGES, FRANK. 1921 - living artist

Born at Wissen in Germany, he has lived in England since 1947. His early training as a jaeger gave him the opportunity to study the wild life of the forests; he was influenced by Wilhelm Buddenberg.
He exhibits in London at the Moorland Gallery.

DOUGLAS, EDWARD ALGERNON STUART. op. 1860-1915

This Victorian, who lived at Barnes, painted many hunting scenes from which it is apparent that he was not a hunting man. Occasionally he painted portraits of horses and dogs and groups such as that of Lord Portman's Hounds.
He exhibited 10 works at R.A. from 1880 onwards.
Coll: Tate, Sydney.

DOUGLAS, EDWIN B. 1848-1907

After studying at the R.A. schools, this Edinburgh man painted animals and sport in the manner of Landseer.
One of his last recorded portraits was of 'Persimmon', the Triple Crown Winner of 1896, in a stable interior.
He exhibited 43 pictures at the R.A. from 1869-1900.

DRAKE, NATHAN., F.S.A. c. 1728-1778

When this son of a Canon of Lincoln arrived in York in 1752, he advertised himself as a landscape painter and drawing-master. An engraving by Grignion of his 'New Walk' – York's Ranelagh Gardens – was made in 1756 but was an improvement on Drake's original painting. He also painted miniatures.
In 1767 he painted the first of 3 pictures for William Joliffe of New Monkton Priory. The portrait of his mounted earth-stopper was followed by one of Jolliffe with his huntsman and hounds and lastly one of his mounted Bailiff. They show more the versatility of this provincial artist than his skill in animal painting. His best portrait was of the York printer, Thomas Gent.
He exhibited 6 works at S.A. and 1 at F.S.
Coll: York A.G.

DREWELL, ROBERT. op. 1844-1860

He lived at Beccles and was employed in painting the portraits of race-horses. He usually showed these with their jockeys up in race-course or landscape settings.

DUBOIS, SIMON. 1660-1708

A Fleming who had been a pupil of Berchem and Wouverman, he came to this country in 1685 and had some success as a portrait painter. Vertue says, 'An incomparable master much better than his brother Edward, (a landscape and history painter), he drew and painted many subjects mighty well, especially horses, cattle, figures, etc.').
He also painted battle-scenes and copied the Old Masters, unashamedly selling these as originals.
Dubois' horses and cattle are painted with the greatest precision. He married a daughter of Van de Velde, the marine painter.

DUPONT, RICHARD J. M. 1920 - living artist
Painter of horses and sporting scenes, he has been patronised by Royalty and has executed commissions for many race-horse owners in Britain, France, and America.
He lives in Essex.
Illustration in B.S.P.

DUDGEON, JAMES. op. 1881-1885
This Victorian painted ordinary hunters in their stables in an ordinary manner.

DUNCAN, EDWARD, R.W.S. 1803-1882
Born in London where his father was an associate of Wm. Huggins the marine painter (not he of Liverpool) whose daughter he was to marry, he was apprenticed to Robt. Havell. He started working on his own as an engraver in aquatint for Huggins and for Fores and produced many plates of race-horses which display a knowledge of anatomy and a good 'eye for a horse'.
He continued to earn his living by engraving until 1844, educating himself meanwhile in painting. He became a popular painter of seascapes, mostly in watercolour, as well as excelling in portraying domestic animals, especially sheep. He illustrated 'Modern Husbandry', which was published in 1852, and did much work for the illustrated papers.
He was elected a member of the Old Society in 1849.
He exhibited 7 works at R.A., 13 at B.I., 12 at S.S., 188 at N.W.C.S., and 332 at O.W.C.S.

*DUNN, J. op. 1846-1851
Nothing is known about this animal painter. 'A White Ox in a Landscape' signed and dated 1846, and an undated 'Chestnut Hunter in a Landscape' are recorded. These works were not of high quality.

DUVAL(L), JOHN. op. 1834-1881
This Ipswich man painted landscape, sporting scenes, equestrian portraits, and portraits of hunters.
He exhibited 18 works at R.A., 10 at B.I., 49 at S.S.
Illustration in B.S.P.

EARL, GEORGE. op. 1856-1883
An animal and sporting painter, he lived in London and Banstead. He painted the occasional portrait.
He exhibited 19 works at R.A., 9 at B.I., and 18 at S.S.

*EARL, MAUD. op. 1884-1919
The daughter of George, she specialised in painting domestic animals, often in the manner of Couldery. She painted the favourite dogs of Victoria and Edward VII and many other pedigree and prize-winning dogs. Her work was much engraved.
She exhibited 3 works at R.A., 1 at S.S.

EARL, THOMAS. op. 1836-1885
This popular painter of dogs and rabbits is thought to be of the same family as George Earl.
He exhibited 47 works at R.A., 62 at B.I., and 108 at S.S.

EARL, THOMAS PERCY. op. 1900-1928
He painted portraits of race-horses from the beginning of this century. Examples are those of 'Sceptre', 1901 Oaks winner, and of the Duke of Portland's 'William III', 1902 Ascot Gold Cup winner. He painted scenes of the Grand National of 1927 and 1928.

EDOUART, A. op. 1815-1816
He is recorded as having submitted from a London address 5 works for exhibition at the R.A. in these 2 years. Three of them were portraits of dogs and one was of a horse.

*EDWARDS, JOHN COLIN. 1940 - living artist
Born at Kidderminster, he studied at the Stourbridge School of Art before going to the R.A. schools where he was a Silver Medallist. He later studied under Annigoni in Florence.
He paints portraits – he was elected a member of the Royal Society of Portrait Painters in 1971 – and draws and paints small and wild animals.
He has exhibited at the R.A. since 1967 and held exhibitions at the Moorland Gallery, London, since 1968.

EDWARDS, LIONEL D. R., R.I.   1878-1966

In the first half of the 20th century, he was deservedly the most popular sporting artist and illustrator of hounds, horses, and hunting in the English sporting periodicals. Whether it was a thumb-nail sketch in pencil of a hound or a hunting scene in oils, here was an artist who knew his subject through and through. He could capture the characteristics of his subjects and they were set in landscape of high artistic merit.

He published 16 books in the course of his long career of which his 'Hunting Sketch Books' and 'Reminiscense of a Sporting Artist' are examples.

EDWARDS, SYDENHAM TEAK.   1768-1819

Born at Usk, Monmouth, he became a distinguished painter of animals and plants. Among his 12 exhibits at the R.A. were 'A Cocking Spaniel', 'Staghounds in Kennel', and a portrait of a 'Hunter with Hounds being Un-kennelled'.

He also painted cattle and game. He illustrated 'The Botanical Magazine'. Scott engraved his 'Lancashire Longhorns' in 1807.

Coll : The V. & A., Kew, and B.M.

EGERTON, DANIEL THOMAS, R.B.A.   op. 1824-d.1842

He painted landscape and some portraits of horses. He travelled and worked in America.

His successful career was brought to an unusually abrupt end by his murder in Mexico.

He exhibited 1 work at B.I. and 65 at S.S.

Illustration in B.S.P.

ELMER, STEPHEN, A.R.A.   1717-1796

A Farnham maltster's son, he continued in the business while gaining a high reputation as a painter of animals, birds, rural scenes, and still life. His bird pictures, especially of game-birds, were true to life, accurately drawn and of artistic merit. Like Charles Collins he could catch the characteristic pose of a bird. He had a bold and free style which gives his paintings individuality.

Some of his best work was of foxhounds and other sporting dogs. He also painted genre.

He became a member of the Society of Aritists in 1763. In 1772 he sent 9 pictures of animals, birds, and fish to the R.A. and was made an A.R.A. He was then considered the most successful British painter of still life and dead game. Many of his pictures were lost in a disastrous fire in 1801.

Daniel's Rural Sports contain 10 engravings by John Scott after him. The Sporting Magazine of 1805 published an engraving of his 'Mallard and French Poodle' and in 1823 one of 'Trojan', a famous foxhound.

He exhibited 117 at R.A. and 113 works at the Free Society.

ELMER, WILLIAM.   op. 1780-1799

As Stephen Elmer was unmarried, it has been assumed naively that William, who lived with him at Farnham, was his nephew. He painted the same subjects in the same style and Grant concedes that, if unsigned, their work is hard to distinguish.

His 'Fox with a Dead Cock Disturbed by Hounds' of 1780 is more lively than the usual work of his uncle.

He visited Ireland and worked there for a time.

He exhibited 6 works at the R.A. between 1783-1799 and 19 at the S.A.

ELSEY, ARTHUR JOHN.   op. from 1878-1893

This painter of genre and animals exhibited between the above dates. His R.A. exhibit of 1878 was a portrait of an Old Pony.

He exhibited 19 works at R.A., 4 at S.S.

Coll : Bournemouth.

ELVERY, JAMES.   op. 1762

A portrait signed and dated 1762 of Richard Rooke on a Hunter accompanied by a hound displays more talent in depicting the man than the animals. These are drawn in the 'primitive' fashion of the day.

EMERY, JAMES.   op. 1779-1822

This actor was an amateur painter of Northern coastal scenes and portraits of horses. He is of interest as being one of the first to paint horses at the New Gallop as distinct from the old rocking-horse style. This had only been tried out before by Seymour with a backckground horse in his picture of 'Lamprey' and by Stubbs in his portrait of 'Baronet'.

He etched a print of the York High Flyer coach after his own picture.

He exhibited 19 works at R.A., of which only two were portraits of horses.

EMMS, JOHN. 1843-1912

Among the dreary numbers of animal painters of his period, the work of this Hampshire artist stands out refreshingly. Devoid of the sentiment that cloyed the work of so many of his contemporaries, his clear and virile style has yet to win the wider recognition that it merits. His portraits of horses display a sound knowledge of anatomy and the ability to 'get' his subject's character. Painting animals and sporting subjects, his predilection was for hounds and dogs. He worked in Ireland for a time.

He exhibited at the R.A. from 1866.

He exhibited 20 works at R.A., 1 at B.I., 51 at S.S.

Coll: Edinburgh.

FEARNSIDE, WILLIAM. op. 1790-1801

This amateur was a landscape and sporting artist. He worked largely in watercolour and exhibited at the N.W.C.S. He exhibited at the R.A. between 1791-1801 as an honorary exhibitor, indicating his amateur status.

He exhibited 8 works at R.A. (drawings).   Coll: 3 in V. & A.

FENN, GEORGE. op. 1833-1840

Work by this provincial painter is scanty and falls into the semi-primitive category. A Chestnut Hunter with foal in a landscape setting, a Galloway Ox in an open landscape, and a Bull in a landscape are recorded. Perhaps he was related to W. W. Fenn, op. 1848-1865, who painted landscape.

He exhibited 1 picture of a dog at the R.A. in 1839.

FERNELEY, CLAUDE LORAINE. 1822-1891

Son of the famous John and named after his god-father, Charles Loraine Smith, his lack of ambition and application prevented him from making more of his talents. His composition was good and he could draw as well as his father, producing some first rate watercolours. He painted hunting scenes and horse portraits in addition to equestrian groups, such as 'A Meet of the Quorn at Kirby Gate'.

He exhibited 1 work at R.A. in 1868 of Horses.

Coll: Leicester A.G.

FERNELEY, JOHN E. 1782-1860

He was the youngest of 6 children of a Leicestershire village carpenter and wheelwright, under whom he worked until he was 21. He used his leisure to school himself in painting and was encouraged by the Duke of Rutland. In 1803 he sent him to London to study under Ben Marshall, with whom he remained for three years, during which time he went to Dover to execute his first commissions for the Leicestershire Militia commanded by the Duke.

In 1806 the R.A. accepted his first exhibits. He started his career in Ireland; married in 1809, and in 1814 settled for the rest of his life in Melton Mowbray where he was so successful that London ceased to be of importance to his fortune. This he made at Melton with his portraits of horses, his 'Hunt Scurries', and set hunting and racing subjects, many of them of large dimensions, in which all the figures of men, horses, and hounds were portraits. Though he could paint a horse as well as Stubbs or Marshall, in other respects, such as composition and perspective, he could be uneven. His friendship with the young Francis Grant improved his figure-painting while in return he improved Grant's painting of horses. He became one of the great sporting artists of the first half of the 19th century, called by Shaw Sparrow the 'Gainsborough of English Horse-painters' because his portraits of well-bred horses have such easy and appealing grace and are handled with such charm that some indifferent figure-painting can be condoned.

He exhibited 22 works at R.A., 4 at B.I., 13 at S.S.

Coll: The Tate, Hull, Leicester and Worthing A.G's and the Mellon Coll.

Illustration in B.S.P.

FERNELEY, JOHN, Jnr. c. 1815-1862

The eldest son of his famous father, in many ways his work was similar, though not so fine.

His earliest work – of a Whipper-in – was engraved for the New Sporting Magazine of May 1833, to be followed the next year by the engraving of a Hunter.

Later he moved to Yorkshire and received commissions from the officers of the Cavalry stationed there. He was most careful to distinguish his work from that of his father, signing himself 'John' against his father's 'J' or adding 'Junior' or 'York' after his signature.

In his horse-portraits the size of the eyes of his subjects are often fashionably exaggerated.

He died in Leeds.

He did not exhibit in London.

Illustration in B.S.P.

FLECKNEY, —   op. 1783
This painter exhibited a picture of an old cart-horse at the Free Society in 1783.

FOLKARD, R. W.   op. 1831-1844
Examples of his work are rare. His 'Mariner', a black greyhound in a landscape setting is dated 1831. This dog won the Swaffham Cup in 1833. A Bay Hunter in a Stable is dated 1844. Perhaps he was the father of the Misses Julia and Elizabeth Folkard who exhibited in the latter part of the century.

FORBES, ALEXANDER, A.R.S.A.   1802-1839
This short-lived Scottish painter was born in Aberdeen. He first made his mark in 1828 by exhibiting 3 pictures at the Scottish Academy while teaching art in Edinburgh. He became Animal Painter to the forerunner of the Royal Highland Agricultural Society and received many commissions for portraits of horses and dogs. These he painted with such sympathy that he earned the then flattering soubriquet of 'Landseer of the North.'

Gilbey considered him an artist of considerable ability who would have reached the front rank of animal-painters had he lived longer.

He exhibited 64 paintings at the Scottish Academy.

FOX, EDWARD M.   op. 1813-1864
He worked in Birmingham, producing portraits of race-horses and hunters, often accompanied by dogs in stable and outdoor settings. He painted in both oils and watercolours. Occasionally he painted prize cattle. He should not be confused with Edward Fox of Brighton who exhibited landscape extensively.

FREEMAN, JAMES.   op. 1828-1858
He painted portraits of horses, often accompanied by dogs and usually in landscape settings. Perhaps he was a member of the Norwich family of that name.

n.b. James Edward Freeman from Nova Scotia painted Italian landscapes.

FRY, WILLIAM THOMAS.   1789-1843
This Londoner was both a painter and an engraver in stipple. The Sporting Magazine of September 1828 published a plate by him of young Lambert Marshall's portrait of his father Ben. In 1827 appeared his print after R. B. Davis of Tom Grant, the Goodwood Huntsman.

He exhibited 3 works at R.A. and 13 works at S.S.

FULTON, SAMUEL.   b. 1855-?
This Glasgow-born artist painted animals, chiefly dogs. His 'Fox-hounds' is in the Glasgow A.G.

Coll: Glasgow A.G.

FURSE, CHARLES WELLINGTON, A.R.A.   1868-1904
Fourth son of an Archdeacon of Westminster and youngest brother of John Furse, the sculptor, from Haileybury he went to the Slade under Legros and then to Julian's in Paris.

Although primarily a portrait-painter, horses were his special love, and play as important a part as the men in his equestrian pictures. He was influenced by Whistler and Sargent. He developed a distinctive and unmistakable style of his own. His first exhibit at the R.A. was in 1888. The following year his portrait of Canon Burrows was received with acclaim. He went on to paint a large number of Mounted M.F.H's. He must be regarded as a forerunner of Munnings. The year before he died of tuberculosis he was made A.R.A. His most famous picture, 'Diana of the Uplands', is in the Tate.

GALE, BENJAMIN. 1741-1832

A native of Hull, he gained his livelihood as a drawing-master and portrait painter. He painted cattle to advertise the products of the local breeder-improvers. It must be suspected that the cattle portrayed were more generously fleshed by his brush than by nature. He also painted marine pieces but did not exhibit. Whessel engraved his 'Driffield Cow' in 1804.

GARLAND, VALENTINE THOMAS. op. 1868-1903

The son of Henry Thomas Garland of Winchester, he worked in oils and watercolour, painting animals and genre.

He exhibited 24 works at the R.A. and at the N.W.C.S.

GARLAND, WILLIAM. op. 1857-d.1882

His painting of a 'Grey Hunter with a Greyhound in a Stable' of 1872, is recorded, but he did not confine himself to animals, painting portraits and landscape. He is believed to have been a brother of Henry: both lived in Winchester.

He exhibited 4 works at R.A.

GARRARD, GEORGE, A.R.A. 1760-1826

This fine artist was both a painter and a sculptor of animals. He studied at the R.A. schools and under Sawrey Gilpin whose daughter he married. He reached his peak as a painter at an early age, his 'View of a Brewhouse Yard' of 1784 being bought by Sir Joshua Reynolds. In addition to work in this genre he painted with power all kinds of horses and cattle, placing them in well executed settings.

He was strongly inclined to sculpture. For his book of 37 coloured aquatints of Improved British Cattle, published in 1800 with the support of the Board of Agriculture, he made models to show the anatomical proportions of the animals. He was elected A.R.A. in 1802. He was much influenced by his friend, Stubbs, and remained on intimate terms with Gilpin who gave him inspiration. After his death in 1807, Garrard turned more and more to sculpture without as much success as he had in painting. In this he was patronised by Lord Egremont and Samuel Whitbread. But he was never advanced to R.A. It must be regretted that he did not stick to his easel.

He exhibited 215 works at R.A., 14 at B.I., and 9 at S.S.

Coll: The Mellon Coll.

Illustration in B.S.P.

GARRARD, R. H. op. 1814

The son of George Garrard, A.R.A., and Matilda, daughter of Sawrey Gilpin, R.A., did not make his mark in the artistic world into which he was bred.

He exhibited only one picture at the R.A. in 1814, a 'Portrait of a Well-known Hunter bred near Worcester, the property of S. Shepherd'.

GAUCI, A. M. op. 1848-1868

He painted and engraved many of the illustrations of celebrated Shorthorn cattle that appeared in 'Coates' Herd Book' between 1863 and 1867. His picture of 'Kate', a Norfolk heifer, dated 1868, is signed 'A. M. Gauci, Animal Painter, Tottenham Court Road'. He is better remembered as an engraver than a painter.

GESSNER, JOHANN CONRAD. 1764-1826

Born in Zurich, he studied at Dresden and visited Italy before coming to England in 1796. He stayed here 8 years. He learnt lithography from its inventor, A. Senefelder. Although he painted some landscape and hunting scenes, his favourite subjects were horses. Among his R.A. exhibits were 'Horses Frightened by Lightning', Horses Frightened by a Bear' and 'Horses Watering by Moonlight'.

He exhibited 24 works at R.A. from 1797-1803.

Coll: V. & A. (drawings), and at B.M.

GILES, GODFREY DOUGLAS, Major. 1857-1941

This professional soldier and amateur artist was born in India and is said to have studied painting in Paris where later he exhibited at the Salon. His earlier works in the 1880's were military scenes in Afghanistan and in the Sudan. These were followed by studies of military uniforms and battle scenes involving horses, depicted, when galloping, in the old fashioned ventre à terre style. His best known picture of this period was 'Saving the Guns at Maiwind'. After his retirement he painted sporting subjects, including a series of Hunts.

He broke new ground by depicting these from the rear, as seen by an ordinary member of the Field, set in a recognisable part of the Hunt's country. He painted many portraits of horses, such as 'Cloister', winner of the 1893 Grand National. He made many illustrations for the Badminton Library volumes on Hunting and on Riding and Polo.

He exhibited 5 works at R.A. from 1884-1888, 1 at S.S., and 1 at the Salon in 1885.

GILES, JAMES WILLIAM, R.S.A. 1801-1870

Born in Glasgow, the son of a textile designer, he studied at the Aberdeen Art School. After an advantageous marriage, he travelled in Italy where he copied Old Masters and painted landscape.

Settling in Aberdeen he started exhibiting in 1828. He became an intimate friend of Landseer with whom he made sketching trips. In order to paint deer – his favourite subject – which he did in great detail, he made himself into an accomplished stalker. Occasionally painting portraits in oils, his preference lay in painting deer and angling subjects.

He was related to John West Giles the lithographer of many sporting scenes and plates of pedigree stock.

Coll: B.M., Aberdeen A.G., The National Gallery of Scotland, and the Melbourne Museum.

GILL, CHARLES. op. 1772-1819

This painter was a pupil of Sir Joshua Reynolds in 1749. Among the 14 portraits that he exhibited at the R.A. were several of animals, such as the 'Spanish Dog and Terrier', an 'Indian Greyhound' and a 'Portrait of a Foxdog'.

GILL, EDWIN. op. 1810-d.1868

There was more than one E. Gill painting in the 19th century. Edwin came to London from Norfolk and worked as a japanner before turning to portraiture and animal painting. About 1823 he left London and settled in Ludlow, and, later, in Hereford where he raised a family of artists.

His early angling and sporting scenes, such as his R.A. exhibit of 1810, 'Evening, Wearied Sportsmen', were often painted with humour. His portrait of 'Osiris', a hunter, is dated 1818. Pollard engraved a set of prints from his 4 colourful and spirited hunting pictures the following year. He also engraved 'The Death Postponed' and three coaching scenes in 1835.

One of his sons was Edmund Marriner ('Waterfall') Gill.

GILLARD, WILLIAM. op. 1850-1856

Believed to have been born in Liverpool about 1812, he is recorded as having worked there, in Dublin, Chester, and London, painting landscape and still life as well as portraits of humans and animals. He exhibited frequently at the Royal Hibernian Academy.

He exhibited 1 work at R.A.

GILPIN, SAWREY, R.A., F.S.A. 1733-1807

The son of a Northumbrian landowner, he was apprenticed to Samuel Scott, the marine painter, in London. Attracted by the work of James Seymour whose drawings he collected and copied, in 1760/61 he produced a set of etchings of different types of horses. He was commissioned by the Duke of Cumberland to paint the portraits of his horses at Newmarket. From there he moved to Windsor and, through his brother William, became friends with Alexander Cozens. A later patron was the rich and eccentric Col. Thornton for whom he painted 'The Death of a Fox'. His treatment of this subject in a realistic manner was a break with tradition and deeply impressed young Ben Marshall at the start of his career as an animal painter. Although this work made his name, Gilpin had ambitions to do more, but his attempts at the popular 'history' subjects were not successful, his 'Election of Darius' and illustrations of Gulliver being the best-known.

Never a rival to Stubbs, 9 years his senior, his work brought a new sense of liveliness and unity of composition; his horses fitted into well-painted landscapes, making the work of his contemporary Francis Sartorius look old-fashioned and primitive. He collaborated with many landscape artists, painting horses and cattle in the compositions of Barratt, Marlow, Zoffany, and Romney. His pupils included John 'Warwick' Smith, Thomas Gooch, and his son-in-law Geo. Garrard.

He was elected President of the Soc. Artists in 1773 and finally an R.A. in 1797. He stands out as an important link in the chain of our great animal painters that stretches from Wootton to Munnings.

He exhibited 36 works at R.A., 83 at S.A., and 1 at B.I.

Coll: The V. & A., Tate, Fitzwilliam, York, Leicester, Nottingham A.G's, and the Mellon Coll.

GODDARD, GEORGE BOUVERIE. 1832-1886
This Wiltshire artist painted animals and sport. At 17 he went to London and taught himself to draw the animals at the Zoo, while earning a living by making sporting drawings for 'Punch' and other papers. On returning to Salisbury he received many commissions but went back to London in 1857, the year after his first R.A. exhibit. Whyte-Melville praised his large 'Lord Wolverton's Bloodhounds' of 1875. His 'Struggle for Existence' of 1879 is in the Walker Gallery, Liverpool.
He died in London.
He exhibited 24 works at R.A. and 3 at S.S.

GOOCH, THOMAS. 1750-1802
Because he was a pupil, with Garrard, of Sawrey Gilpin, it is surprising that Gooch did not become a better animal-painter. His style appears to have been based on James Seymour; Shaw Sparrow aptly calls him a semi-primitive. His handling of the landscape, in which his usual subjects of horses and dogs are set, is frequently of far higher artistic quality than that of the subjects themselves and clearly shows the influence of his master.
He exhibited at the Society of Artists from 1772 and at the R.A. from 1781. He was one of the first to portray 'The Life of a Racehorse' in six stages, exhibited in 1783, which he later engraved himself. But few of his works were engraved during his lifetime. In 1800 when he had retired from London to Lyndhurst, he painted the famous Ox who won a race there of nearly 2 miles in 8 minutes.
He exhibited 76 works at the R.A., 4 at S.A., 1 at F.S.
Coll: Mellon Coll.
Illustration in B.S.P.

GOODE, JOHN. c. 1810-c.1865
The work of this Adderbury man is rare. His large equestrian group of 1852 of the Old Berkshire Hounds with their huntsman and two whippers-in was engraved in mezzotint by P. Thomas: the portraits of men, horses, and hounds are of good quality. A portrait of a Shorthorn Cow is at Reading University.
He exhibited 2 sporting pictures at S.S. in 1835.

GRAEME (ROE), COLIN. 1858-1910
One of the sons of R. H. Roe (q.v.) he dropped his surname to distinguish himself from other members of his family but his talents hardly justified this step. He painted commonplace portraits of horses, dogs on the moors, and terriers with rabbits. Even a 'Waiting for Master' is recorded.

GRANT, Sir FRANCIS, P.R.A. 1803-1878
Fourth son of a Scottish laird, he was born in Edinburgh and educated at Harrow. Passionately devoted to fox-hunting and to painting, he spent his patrimony on the former at Melton but more than recouped it there with his brush. At 31 his circumstances forced him to turn professional. He received some instruction in painting from his hunting friend Ferneley, whose influence can be detected in his work. He was apt at 'getting a likeness' with humans and could give his horses character.
Handsome, well-connected, and with charming manners, he rapidly attracted notice with his equestrian groups, many of which were engraved. 'The Melton Hunt Breakfast' became the best known. His picture of Queen Victoria riding with Lord Melbourne in Windsor Park made him the most sought-after portrait painter of the day, and for the rest of his life he exhibited regularly at the R.A.
He was elected A.R.A. in 1842 and full R.A. in 1851. After Landseer's refusal of the honour, he was elected P.R.A. in 1865, a position that he filled to perfection.
Although primarily a portrait-painter, the well-painted animals in his sporting compositions merit his inclusion here.
He exhibited 253 works at R.A., 7 at B.I., 9 at S.S.

GRAY, —. op. 1783
The Free Society of Artists exhibited in 1783 two pictures of horses and two others by this artist whose initials were not recorded.

GRIMSTONE, E. op. 1837-1897
This portrait painter produced some pictures of dogs and other animals, such as 'Bloodhound and Whelps',

'The Dying Hound', the 'Death of Grafton, the Celebrated Bloodhound', all exhibited at the R.A. between 1837-1879, together with three other animal subjects and nine portraits.
He lived at Ealing.

GWYNNE, WILLIAM.   op. 1795-1838
This Shropshire man worked at Ludlow, painting horses, cattle and pigs. His 'Shropshire Pig' was engraved by W. Wright in 1795. 'A light bay horse in a landscape' was dated 1838.

HACKERT, JOHANN GOTTLIEB.   1744-1773
One of five brothers, who included James Philip (Philippe) 1737-1807, and George, 1755-1805, they were the sons of a Prussian portrait-painter. With his brothers he studied under le Seur in Berlin before going to Rome from whence he and Philippe sent exhibits to the S.A. Johann specialised in animal painting. He came to England in 1772.
Among his 9 exhibits at the R.A. next year was 'Four Hounds'. Later that year he died at Bath.
He exhibited 9 works at R.A., and 40 works at S.A.

HAIGH, ALFRED G.   1870-1962
This sound horse-painter could portray race-horses more artistically than many of his contemporaries. He worked at Newmarket. He painted a double portrait of the Duke of Portland's 'Phaleron' and 'Primer' with their jockeys.

HALL, HARRY.   op. 1838-1886
This first class draughtsman of hunters and thoroughbreds occasionally produced portraits and shooting scenes. He was a second rate artist described by Shaw Sparrow as Herring's 'echo'. He did some work in London but lived mostly at Newmarket where, like a present-day photographer, he was employed in taking the likenesses of innumerable race-horses. This he did with great exactitude so that his work is of value to historians of the Turf. He was extremely industrious and much of his work was engraved, the Old Sporting Magazine publishing 114 of his plates. His work still remains popular.
He exhibited 11 works at R.A., 17 at B.I., 26 at S.S.
Coll : Mellon Coll., Burnley and Cheltenham A.G's.
Illustration in B.S.P.

HAMILTON, CHARLES.   op. 1831-1867
Living at Kensworth, he painted hounds, horses, and cattle as well as sporting and many oriental scenes. His portrait of the huntsman Robert Oldaker with his pack and Whippers-in was shown at the R.A. in 1837 and the Kensworth Harriers in 1838.
He exhibited 12 works at R.A., 22 at B.I., 12 at S.S.

HAMILTON-RENWICK, LIONEL.   1919 - living artist
This artist lives near Newmarket and paints race-horses and equestrian portraits. He studied at Heatherleys. He has received commissions from Royalty and many prominent owners to paint portraits of their horses, such as 'Santa Claus', 1964 Derby winner, and 'Ragusa'. He painted the portrait of Her Majesty's 'Aureole'.

HANCOCK, CHARLES.   1795-1868
Born at Marlborough, on the downs of which many fine race-horses have been trained, he started his painting career there. He moved to Reading, and then on to London where he became a constant attendant at Tattersall's Sale-yard. He started exhibiting in London in 1819. It speaks well for his talents as a painter of horses, hounds, dogs, prize cattle, and of sporting scenes that he was well-patronised at a time when such high-flyers as Herring, Pollard, Agasse, and Abraham Cooper were in their prime.
He exhibited 23 works at R.A., 55 at B.I., 47 at S.S.
Coll : Tate, Glasgow A.G.

HAND, THOMAS.   c.1771-d.1804
Hand became a pupil and assistant to Geo. Morland in his Camden Town period of 1787. To say that he was a more successful imitator of his Master's amusements than of his painting does not do him full justice. He could imitate Morland's work nearly to perfection but Grant found that close examination revealed a slighter, hastier technique and certain yellow and red pigments, not used by Morland, that gave his work a gayer aspect. His choice of rustic subjects were identical to those of Morland to whom much of Hand's work has been attributed.

He died six weeks before his old Master and drinking companion.
He exhibited 21 works at R.A. and 1 at S.A.

HARDMAN, J. op. 1812-1846
This painter sent from Finsbury two pictures of horses to the R.A. in 1812, 'Worthy' and 'Elizabeth' and her colt, both the property of the Honourable East India Company. A Bay Hunter in a Stable was dated 1846.

HARDY, HEYWOOD. 1843-1933
This still popular painter, brother of James, worked in both oils and watercolour. That he could paint fine portraits of horses is shown by his picture of 'Glenside' with J. R. Anthony up, winner of the 1911 Grand National. These are rarer than his fancy pictures of mounted 18th century gallants sweeping off their tricornes to chance-met Dianas. The horses that they ride are still well-painted, though this may not be apparent in the reproductions that adorn the lids of innumerable chocolate boxes.
He exhibited 31 works at R.A., 9 at B.I., 16 at S.S., 7 at O.W.C.S.
Coll: V. & A.
Illustration in B.S.P.

HARDY, JAMES Jnr., R.I. 1832-1889
This popular Victorian artist, who lived in Bristol, jumped aboard the Balmoral bandwaggon driven by Landseer, to produce many Scottish sporting scenes in which live animals, tended by dour ghillies, predominate over the dead bag to hand. Both figures and landscape settings were painted well enough and bore such titles as 'On the Moors' or 'Tying up the Game'. His compositions now have a certain antimacassar-period charm.
He worked in watercolours as well as in oils.
He exhibited 9 works at R.A., 8 at B.I., 46 at S.S., 28 at N.W.C.S.
Coll: the V. & A.
Illustration in B.S.P.

HARGREAVES, JOHN. op.1834
A work is recorded by this painter of the grey stallion 'Essence', with a bay hunter, two hounds, and a groom, in a wooded landscape.

HARRINGTON, R. 1800-1882
This pupil of Abraham Cooper worked at Carlisle, painting cattle and horses. A picture of a saddled bay pony with two dogs in a loose-box is recorded. Thomas Fairland lithographed some of his work, such as the heifer 'Eden'.

HARROWING, WALTER. op. 1880-1904
This horse-painter executed commissions to paint the portraits of hunters.

HASELER, W. op. 1859-1860
Living in Bath, he submitted 3 pictures of cattle to S.S. in the above years.

HERBERTE, E. B. op 1860-1893
This sporting artist was active in the last half of the 19th century. He produced many hunting scenes painted in a stiff and starchy style that reflect unconsciously the formal manners of that epoch. His portraits of hunters are well done and disclose a finer knowledge of the horse than his hunts would suggest. He painted 'Frigate's' Grand National of 1889 with the field jumping Beecher's Brook.
He did not exhibit in London
Illustration in B.S.P.

HERRING, BENJAMIN, Snr. 1806-1830
The younger brother of the famous J. F., his work is rare as he died young. One, a copy of Marshall's picture of 'Longwaist' dated 1827, and another after Marshall, might indicate that he was his pupil. A coaching scene and a chestnut hunter with groom in a landscape are recorded among his output.
He did not exhibit.

HERRING, BENJAMIN, Jnr. 1830-1871
The youngest son of the famous J.F. whose favourite he was, he had not the talent of his brother Charles nor

the ambition of his brother John. His output was not large and he died young. He painted animals and sporting scenes. He lived at Tonbridge.

He exhibited 4 pictures at the B.I. from 1861 to 1863 and 2 at S.S.

HERRING, CHARLES. 1828-1856

The most talented of J. F. Herring's three sons, he predeceased his father by nine years. They worked in collaboration and Herring Senior was not above signing his name to Charles' work, thus denying him due recognition. His favourite subjects were farmyards in which all the usual farm animals and poultry figure. He exhibited 1 work at S.S.

*HERRING, JOHN FREDERICK, Snr. 1795-1865

The son of a London fringe-maker, he started his working life as a coach painter before becoming a driver of stage coaches in Yorkshire. During this 7-year period he developed his natural ability to draw horses and to study their anatomy. After leaving the road, he studied for a short time as a pupil of Abraham Cooper, his only formal training in art.

He gained rapid success in painting portraits of horses and especially winners on the Turf, going on to paint, in all, 18 Derby winners and 33 successive winners of the St. Leger. Reproductions of his work in colour proved extremely popular. Save for Henry Alken, he became the best-known sporting artist of his day, though lacking Alken's humour.

He painted many sporting and country scenes, often set in actual localities, but fewer coaching scenes than one would expect. He received commissions from Geo. IV, Will. IV and Queen Victoria and was appointed Animal Painter to the Duchess of Kent. Devoted to Landseer, he retained his own style, however, which for an ex-whip and pupil of Cooper might have been more robust. He was only slightly affected by the Victorian blight of sentimentality which is reflected in the well-fed condition of the animals and poultry in his many farmyard scenes – a far cry from Morland's work-weary horses and age-worn cows. He also painted attractive small pictures of domestic animals. He remains one of the most generally popular, if not the most talented, of our animal painters.

He exhibited 22 works at R.A., 82 at S.S. The Old Sporting Magazine published 49 reproductions of his work.

Coll: Brighton, Liverpool, Birkenhead, Leeds, Hull, Nottingham, Leicester, Newcastle, York A.G's.

HERRING, JOHN FREDERICK, Jnr. 1815-1907

A younger son of his famous father, to whom he was apupil, he had not the talent but more ambition than his brother Charles and broke away from parental control. He had no scruples, however, in signing his work 'J. F. Herring' and as this was in style and subject nearly identical to his father's, as much confusion has been caused as with the two Henry Alkens. Shaw Sparrow detects inferior composition and a certain hardness of outline in his work compared to that of Herring Senior.

He painted many scenes of field sports in watercolour and farmyard scenes in oils. He exhibited 3 works at R.A., 10 at B.I., 53 at S.S.

HIGTON, THOMAS. op. 1801-1815

This forgotten artist's 'forte' was painting portraits of dogs, for which he was employed by Lords Warwick and Sedley. He also exhibited land and sea-scapes and included horses and cattle among his subjects. He exhibited 15 works at R.A. between the above dates.

HILLS, ROBERT, R.W.S. 1769-1844

Born at Islington, Hills was a pupil of John Gresse and became a distinguished and prolific painter of animals in watercolours. His talents as an etcher have not received their due, while examples of his sculpture brought high praise in his day and regrets that he did not pursue this branch of the arts more vigorously. But vigour was not in character: his favourite subjects were deer, which he was often called on to insert in other men's works. He made a series of 780 etchings of animals from 1798 to 1815.

He exhibited 44 works at R.A., 2 at B.I., and 600 at O.W.C.S. of which he was a foundation member.

Coll: V. & A., Cardiff, Fitzwilliam, Manchester and etchings at B.M.

HILTON, T. op. 1805

This artist, who lived in York, painted the portrait of the race-horse 'Haphazard' from which J. Whessel made an engraving.

HINCKLEY, THOMAS HEWES. 1813-1896

He was a native of Boston, U.S.A. His picture of a Boston Spaniel with a Dead Snipe was well composed and worthy of note. He sent 2 paintings of dogs with game to the R.A. in 1858 – 'Setters at Rest' and 'Setters at Point'.

HOBART, J. P. op. 1857-1858

'A Bay Hunter and Foxhounds' in a landscape and 'Hunters in their Stables' are works by this painter.

HODGES, WALTER PARRY (né Parry). 1760-1845

This long-lived and gifted amateur was Receiver-General for the County of Dorset and is known for his hunting scenes, painted in watercolour. A popular set of 8 of the Beaufort Hunt were engraved by Henry Alken and published in 1833. 'The Chase' and the 'Death of a Roebuck' followed the next year and two of Hare Hunting were published in 1836 – all engraved by Reeve. Strictly, he should be regarded as a sporting rather than an animal painter.

HONDIUS, ABRAHAM. c.1638-1695

Coming to London from Rotterdam about 1666, he remained here for the rest of his life painting animals. One of the first foreigners to influence our native artists in this field, he brought with him a frank realism and a sound knowledge of anatomy. Horace Walpole remarked that his manner was his own, bold and free, and thought few masters, except Rubens and Snyders, had painted animals in so great a style. Vertue praised his paintings of bull-baiting and his famous 'Dog Market' which showed dogs of 30 different breeds.
He became more than a painter of animals, turning his hand with great artistic effect to portraits and hunting scenes, done with a smoother technique than the former, until gouty old age took toll of his talents.
His 'Hunting the Porcupine' was engraved and published in the Sporting Magazine (vol. 22) in 1804.
Coll: Fitzwilliam Museum (3), Glasgow (1) and Wolverhampton (1).

HOPKINS, WILLIAM H. op. 1853-d.1892

This Keynsham landscape artist painted animals, rural and sporting scenes and animals. He painted the portraits of the Prince Consort's two favourite hunters. He collaborated with Edmund Havell, who painted the figures to produce pictures of Her Majesty's Buck-hounds in 1876 and the Fitzwilliam Hounds in 1888.
He exhibited 37 works at R.A., 21 at B.I., and 24 at S.S.
Coll: Bristol A.G.

HORLOR, GEORGE W. op. 1849-1891

This Victorian painted landscape, in which animals predominated, in the popular Balmoral manner, as well as portraits of animals and sporting scenes.
His R.A. exhibits included such subjects as 'Collie Dog and Rabbit', the 'Shepherd's Dogs', 'Sporting Dogs', and a 'Shooting Pony'. He worked at Cheltenham, Birmingham, and Brentford.
He exhibited 19 works at R.A., 35 at B.I., and 33 at S.S.
Collection: Cheltenham A.G.

*HORNER, GEORGE CHRISTOPHER. 1829-1881

Painting animals and genre, he worked in Manchester, Birmingham, Brentford and London. He painted 'Macomo and his Friends' the celebrated Zulu lion- tamer in a cageful of lions. Charles Turner engraved his portrait of the heifer, 'Yorkshire Rose'.
He exhibited at the B.I. from 1857 to 1867.

HOWARD, FRANK. 1805-1866

Son of Henry Howard, R.A., and pupil to him and to Lawrence, he painted portraits and some lion hunts as well as the mythological subjects of his sire. Surprisingly he painted 'Dangerous', Derby winner of 1833; this was aquatinted by E. Duncan.
In 1840 he published 'Game and Wild Animals of Southern Africa'.
He exhibited 43 works at R.A., 26 at B.I., and 9 at S.S.

HOWE, JAMES. 1780-1836

Born at Skirling, Peeblesshire, where his father was Minister, he was apprenticed to a house painter in Edinburgh but took to drawing animals. The Highland Society of Scotland commissioned him to paint a series of

38

portraits of well-known animals to promote improved breeding. Sir John Sinclair commissioned him to draw examples of various breeds of cattle. Lizars published and engraved many of his 14 drawings of horses in 1824. A series of 45 engravings of his horses and cattle was published in 1832.

He lived in Edinburgh, only going to London once to paint the horses of the Royal Stud. In 1815 he visited the field of Waterloo, and exhibited his picture of the Battle at the R.A. in 1816.

In 1834 Charles Turner mezzotinted his 'Hawking', an outstanding work.

He exhibited at the Royal Institute and R.S.A. from 1808.

HOWITT, SAMUEL. 1765-1822

In reaction to his Quaker upbringing his work reflected his light-hearted, adventurous character. Early independance while he lived at Chigwell allowed him to take part in all field sports. This experience he used to full advantage when forced to turn professional and set up as a drawing-master in London where he became a court card in Rowlandson's pack.

He worked in watercolour and oils and was a prolific etcher of sporting scenes.

He illustrated 'The Anglers' Manual' in 1808 and produced 56 plates for 'A New Work of Animals' in 1811, his designs inspired by Aesop's Fables. In 1812, 70 of his illustrations appeared in 'The British Sportsman'. On the authority of the D.N.B. he never travelled abroad but this was no bar to his illustrating 'Oriental Field Sports' published in 1817; his designs were made from sketches drawn by his friend Capt. Williamson. The Old Sporting Magazine published in all 157 of his engravings.

His marriage to Rowlandson's favourite sister was not a success – his passion for fishing excursions leaving her high and dry – and they lived apart during their later years.

He exhibited only 10 works at R.A., and 3 at S.A.

Coll : V. & A., B.M., Manchester.

HUBBARD, B. op. 1839-1864

This Lincolnshire painter lived at Louth and gained a livelihood painting portraits of horses and dogs, often with those of their owners. He painted the Trusthorpe Ox. Moody engraved his Prize Heifer 'Flower'.

He exhibited 7 works at the R.A., including 2 of ponies and 1 of a spaniel.

HUBBARD, CHARLES. op. c.1840

One of the early painters of pedigree cattle, he lived at Louth, Lincs. It is presumed that he was the father of B. Hubbard.

*HUGGINS, WILLIAM. 1820-1884

Born in Liverpool 18 years after Landseer and 25 years after Herring, this artist ranks among the more important animal painters of his century : his technique was to influence such men as Joseph Crawhall (b.1861). He studied art at the Liverpool Mechanic's Institute. At the start of his career he produced pictures of literary and religious narrative subjects but he became fascinated sketching the lions and tigers in the Chester Zoo. His first exhibit at the R.A. in 1842, 'Androcles and the Lion' contained the clue to his future development. About 1860 he rebelled against the conventional use of impasto, and using smooth white mill board, glazed it with rich transparent pigments through which the white background showed luminously, as Turner had done with his watercolours. This was a startling contrast to the age-old practice of painting in oils from a dark background to light.

A small touchy man, like Turner, he bravely withstood the scorn of his critics and continued to produce accomplished pictures of lions, tigers, and other cats with vigour and sensibility. He might be termed the Head of our Feline School.

He exhibited 31 works at R.A. and 8 at B.I.

Coll : Birkenhead, Walker, Preston A.G's.

HULK, WILLIAM F. op. 1875-1906

An animal and landscape painter who lived near Guildford, he painted, in oils and watercolour, cattle and sheep in Surrey scenery.

He exhibited 45 works at R.A., 43 at S.S., and 13 at N.W.C.S.

*HUNT, EDGAR. c.1873-1955

The son of Walter Hunt, Jnr., he painted birds, animals, and fruit pieces. His compositions, usually on small canvasses, were mostly of farmyard scenes in which domestic poultry and their broods predominated; though calves, goats, pigs and rabbits were also introduced. He worked in a meticulous manner – not a feather or a hair was out of place.

He was of a retiring disposition and seldom exhibited, spending his life with the animals that he owned and constantly painted. His work has become extremely popular.

HUNT, WALTER. b.1861-1931

He was the son of Walter, Snr., and father of Edgar Hunt. All three were animal painters and lived in Warwickshire. He went further afield for his subjects than Edgar, including sporting scenes in his œuvre. Among his 19 exhibits at the R.A. in 1888 he showed 'Otter Hunting – the Find', in 1894, 'Bolting the Otter', in 1896, 'Off the Scent', in 1901, 'Breaking Cover', and in 1910 'Otter Hounds in Full Cry'.

His 'Dog in the Manger' of 1885 was bought for the Chantrey Bequest.

Coll: Leeds, Tate.

*HURT, LOUIS BOSWORTH. 1859-1929

Shaggy Highland cattle with their sweeping horns were the speciality of this Derbyshire painter. These he set in their picturesque habitat beside lochs and burns among heathery hills. Occasionally he ventured to depict sheep in the same kind of setting. He must be regarded as much a landscape as an animal painter.

He exhibited 13 works at R.A., 26 at S.S.

Coll: Manchester A.G.

IBBETSON, JULIUS CAESAR. 1759-1817

Strictly, this minor Master of English Landscape should have no place in a volume of animal painters, but his cattle-pieces and a volume of his watercolour drawings of animals display his natural sympathy with them, so that he cannot be ommitted.

INGPEN, A. W. op. 1830-1839

Little is known about this animal painter whose work appears in the sale-room infrequently: perhaps he died young – it seems that he lived in Canterbury. His first exhibit at the R.A. in 1834 was a portrait of a hackney, followed the next year by that of a hunter. In 1836 he showed 'Mameluke', the Derby winner of 1827. One of his B.I. exhibits in 1833 was of 'Two Hounds'.

He exhibited 8 works at R.A. of which 5 were horses; 2 of dogs at B.I., and 6 at S.S.

JACKSON, GEORGE. op. 1830-1864

The work of this good provincial artist is gradually coming to light and must be regarded with respect. His portraits of animals, set in finely-painted and varied landscapes, show his sound knowledge of anatomy.

His first recorded work was of 'Two Pointers', dated 1833: his only exhibit at the R.A. was of 'Dead Game' in 1844. He was most prolific in the 1860's, painting the portraits of many hunters, sometimes accompanied by dogs. One of these, painted at Wadhurst, Kent, gives the only clue to his possible locality.

He exhibited 1 work at R.A. in 1844.

Illustration in Shaw Sparrow's Sporting Painters.

JOHNSON, F. op. 1791-1797

He sent to the Society of Artists in 1791, from Croydon, portraits of a race-horse, a road-horse, and a phæton pony.

He sent a picture of snipe to the R.A. in 1797 as an honorary exhibitor, indicating that he was regarded as an amateur.

JONES, A. R.

This Manchester man painted cattle and dogs. He sent a picture of the former to the B.I. in 1845.

*JONES, CHARLES. 1836-1892

The youngest son of S. J. E. Jones, he studied under his father. In youth his friendship with a vet. ready to correct his anatomy studies furthered his interest in painting animals. From the age of 21 he spent 6 years on a farm at Maidenhead painting animals and landscape. After his return to work in London, he made annual visits to Scotland and became as well-known for his Highland scenes as for his pictures of cattle and sheep: he was nicknamed 'Sheep' Jones. Though a good horseman and shot, he rarely painted sporting subjects.

His work is characterised by a high finish, but later in life he broadened his effects and used more brilliant colours. He was a typical Victorian artist with the qualities and defects of his age.

He exhibited 12 at R.A., 12 at B.I., and 61 at S.S.

Coll: Cardiff.

JONES, PAUL. op. 1856-1879

The favourite subjects of this painter, a son of S. J. E. Jones, were terriers, either ratting or rabbiting. His pictures were small in size and sometimes painted on panel. His subjects included stalking scenes with the usual ghillies, ponies, and dogs.

JONES, RICHARD. 1767-1840

A native of Reading, he first exhibited at the B.I. in 1810. In 1818 he sent to the R.A. the portrait of a bull, 'Emperor'. The following year he moved to a studio in Leicester Square to be near his friend Abraham Cooper. He sent 3 works to the R.A. in 1819 and 7 in 1820, after which he sent no more – due perhaps to his great independance of character.

In 1824 he was living in Louth and painting portraits of cattle. By 1830 he had moved to Birmingham where he painted the portrait of the St. Leger winner of that year.

Coll: Walker A.G.

JONES, SAMUEL JOHN EGBERT. op. 1820-1855

This popular and prolific artist, the father of Charles and Paul, produced many scenes of shooting, angling, and coaching as well as painting pure landscape and occasional portraits of humans and horses. His landscape, by itself or as a setting for his sporting figures, is well-painted and commands respect, being far superior to that of most animal painters, amongst whom he can hardly be numbered. His work was much engraved by Charles and George Hunt, Fellows, Hineley, Pyall, and Smart.

He exhibited 14 works at R.A., 14 at B.I., and 19 at S.S.

JOSI, CHARLES, R.B.A. op. 1827-1851

He became a popular painter of animals which often filled his entire canvas. His portrait of the Bay Arab presented to William IV by the Imam of Muscat was exhibited in 1843 at the R.A. where he also exhibited several pictures of dogs.

He exhibited 9 works at R.A. of which 7 were of animals, 12 at B.I., and 53 at S.S.

KEELING, E. J. op. 1856-1873

Work by this Victorian painter is rare. He produced in 1858 an equestrian picture of 2 hunting men accompanied by 2 couples of hounds. Other recorded works of 1861 were of 2 pointers with a sportsman in a moorland setting and of Shetland ponies in a landscape. He painted some portraits of horses. Perhaps he was a son of W. K. Keeling, R.I., of Manchester.

He did not exhibit in London.

KEMP-WELCH, LUCY ELIZABETH, R.I. 1869-1958

Born at Bournemouth, she studied art at the Herkomer School at Bushey where she settled, devoting herself to painting animals, especially horses. She first exhibited at the R.A. in 1894 and thereafter regularly for many years. Her 'Colt Hunting in the New Forest' of 1897 was bought by the Chantrey Bequest which later acquired her 'Forward, the Guns' of 1917. Her 'Timber-hauling in the New Forest' of 1904, in the Bristol A.G., well displays her powers of composition, of colouring, and of her observation of heavy horses straining at their work in characteristic if unconventional attitudes.

Coll: The Tate, Melbourne, Bournemouth, Bristol, and Exeter A.G's.

KEYL, FRIEDRICK WILHELM. 1823-1871

This painter, of German origin, was a pupil and studio assistant to Landseer and was much patronised by Queen Victoria, painting portraits and pictures of animals on the royal farms, such as the Hereford Bullock and Lambs in Windsor Home Park. He painted 'Lootie', a Pekinese presented to Her after the Sack of Pekin; this he exhibited at the R.A. in 1862. Almost completely forgotten today, he was true to his sentimental age inserting with delicate care in the settings of his cattle portraits, ducks, song-birds, or sweet little kittens. In these canvasses he displayed more talent than was shown by many of his better-known contemporaries.

He exhibited 34 works at the B.I. from 1850-66, and 42 at the R.A. from 1847-72.

Coll: Royal Coll.

KILLINGBECK, BENJAMIN. op. 1769-1796
This painter and mezzotinter is believed to have been born in Leeds and to have begun his career as a portrait-painter. He was commissioned by Lord Rockingham and other noblemen to paint portraits of their horses. These are set in well-painted landscapes and show the influence of Stubbs. He produced pictures of game-birds and sporting scenes. He engraved a mezzotint of the race-horse 'Highflyer', which was also painted by Sawrey Gilpin.
He exhibited 11 works at R.A., all of animals and birds; 12 at S.A.; 28 at F.S.

KINCH, H. op. 1811-1824
A Fareham man, he was a painter of horses, hunting scenes, and landscape. His exhibits included portraits of hunters, hackneys, and ponies.
He exhibited 17 works at R.A., of which 11 were of horses.

KING, JOHN. 1929 - living artist
Born near Salisbury, he was trained at that city's School of Art and was a pupil of Lionel Edwards. He exhibits annually at the Wildlife Society Exhibition, his subjects including deer, foxes, and hounds. He has painted the portraits of such famous race-horses as Mill House, Arkle, Nijinsky, and Mill Reef.
He has held exhibitions in London.

KNYFF, LEONARD. 1650-1721
Born in Amsterdam, he came to England about 1712 and was employed in making topographical drawings of the seats of the nobility and gentry; these were engraved by John Kip for the 'Britannia Illusrata'. Some of these bird's-eye views he reproduced in oils of large size, supposedly for the subjects' owners. He was later employed by Lord Halifax to paint pictures of his animals. His rare work, such as 'Blackgame and Rabbits, with Swallows', is more spacious than the overcrowded compositions of his contemporary, Francis Barlow.
Coll: Leeds A.G.

LAMBERT, JAMES. 1725-1788 'of Lewes'
Born at Eastbourne, he pursued his career as an instructor of both music and painting at Lewes, being known as Lambert 'of Lewes'. His style in landscape painting closely resembles that of his neighbours the brothers Smith 'of Chichester'. His pictures usually included cattle or sheep.
He received many commissions from local breeders to portray their prize-animals. He visited Devon in 1762, but it is believed that he never worked in London.
He exhibited 7 works at R.A. including 'Mr. Bakewell's Famous Ram' in 1774; 17 at S.A., and 30 at F.S.

LAMBERT, J. W. op. 1822-1851
This animal and sporting painter worked in Surrey and Sussex. He painted landscape there and in France At B.I. he showed in 1823 a 'Shooting Pony and Pointer' and in 1839 'Sheepwashing', while at the R.A. in 1836 he showed 'The Surrey Foxhounds Breaking Cover', the figures depicted being portraits.
He exhibited 9 works at R.A., 4 at B.I., 11 at S.S.

LANDSEER, CHARLES, R.A. 1799-1879
Middle son of John, the engraver, he produced a few pictures of animals amongst his large and popular output of history and genre subjects. In 1838 he showed at B.I. 'Two Puppies and a Kitten'. His 'Blood-hound and Pups' is in the Tate.
He exhibited 73 works at R.A., 26 at B.I., 11 at S.S.

*LANDSEER, Sir EDWIN HENRY, R.A. 1802-1873
The third and youngest son of John Landseer, A.R.A., the engraver, his precocious talent that made him the most famous animal painter of his period, became apparent at an early age. From the start he was drawn to sketching animals, sometimes in company with the young J. F. Lewis. He received encouragement from Haydon and was influenced by James Ward and Stubbs, whose drawings for 'The Anatomy of A Horse', he later acquired. His first exhibit at the R.A. was accepted when he was 12 years old. In 1818 his 'Fighting Dogs getting Wind' exhibited there made his name and thenceforth he exhibited regularly.
In 1824 he went to the Highlands with C. R. Leslie and returned there year after year to paint its scenery and life. He achieved quick success both in his profession and with Society. His small Highland landscapes of the 1820's and 1830's are his best, and a revelation to those who only know his later work. He was elected

A.R.A. in 1826 and full R.A. in 1831. The young Queen Victoria's preference for sketches and freely-painted pictures made him one of her favourite artists.

The Germanic sentimentality of the Prince Consort, however, influenced the Queen's taste and Landseer's style became more highly-finished. He was much employed painting portraits of the Royal children and animals at Balmoral and Osborne. He taught the Royal couple to etch. Superb draughtsman and anatomist though he was, capable of painting animals with vigour and true insight, his unfortunate ability to portray them with human feelings while adorning a moral, met the eager demand of his Royal and other patrons. These products, in which stags were favourite subjects, were engraved by his brother Thomas and met a ready market throughout the far-flung Empire and beyond.

When he was buried in St. Paul's Cathedral, the four lions that he had sculpted for the base of Nelson's Column in Trafalgar Square wore black wreaths round their neck.

Had this fashionable and lucrative blight not halted him in mid-career, his talents might have made him a painter of real European importance. In 1865 he was elected P.R.A. but refused the honour due to ill health. He exhibited 179 works at R.A., 94 at B.I., 4 at S.S.

Coll: V. & A., Tate, Walker, Manchester, Bedford, Bournemouth, Nottingham, Newcastle A.G's.

Illustration in B.S.P.

LANDSEER, THOMAS, A.R.A.   1795-1880

The elder brother of the famous Edwin, they were both instructed in engraving by their father, John Landseer, and by B. R. Haydon. He remained in closest sympathy with Edwin whose fame he greatly enhanced, engraving practically all his work – strictly he has no place in this volume.

LAPORTE, GEORGE HENRY, R.I.   1799-1873

Born in Hanover, the son of John Laporte the landscapist artist whose influence shows in the settings of his pictures, he became a popular painter of horses and dogs. These were done from close observation and in the greatest detail in the style beloved by Victorian sportsmen. He worked in both oils and watercolour and was an original member of the New Water Colour Society. He was appointed Animal Painter to the Duke of Cumberland.

The Old Sporting Magazine published in all 43 plates from his work covering a wide variety of animal and sporting subjects. Fores published a set of 4 plates of his Liverpool Steeplechase of 1839. His illustrations for sporting books were engraved by the best engravers.

In step with his times, he produced romantic compositions, of Cavaliers, Arabs, and military scenes in which horses predominated.

He exhibited 9 works at R.A., 21 at B.I., 18 at S.S., 136 at N.W.C.S.

Illustration in B.S.P.

LAWRENCE, RICHARD.   op. 1793-1816

This Birmingham veterinary surgeon was a painter and sculptor of sufficient merit to have his work accepted for exhibition by the R.A. and B.I.

In 1793 he sent to the R.A. portraits of two horses at the Veterinary College: in 1807, 'A Stag Swimming' and a 'Portrait of the Celebrated Durham Ox': in 1814 portraits of 2 hunters belonging to Lord Middleton. In 1815 he sent to the B.I. A Greek Equestrian vaulting onto his horse, and in 1816 a Model of an Arab Horse, which was intended to be part of an Equestrian statue of the Duke of Wellington.

*LEAR, EDWARD.   1812-1888

The inclusion in this volume of this landscape artist and endearing writer of nonsense is justified by the watercolour drawings of animals made for Lord Stanley from specimens in the private zoo at Knowsley. Between 1832 and 1837 he produced a Volume of 108 watercolour drawings of birds, animals, and a turtle collected there, of which 'An Antelope' and 'A Wallaby' are examples.

Coll: Bedford A.G.

*LEAVERS, LUCY A.   op. 1887-1898

This Nottingham lady specialised in painting with great exactitude pictures of dogs and cats and their progeny. Often on large canvasses she devised dramatic domestic situations such as 'The Antagonist' – a terrier barking at a kitten on a wheelbarrow, or 'An Anxious Moment' in which a puppy is about to be

stung by bees from a damaged hive. One can almost read the names engraved on the collars of the participating terriers. This picture was shown at the R.A. in 1895, to which she sent 6 others.
Coll: Nottingham A.G.

LEIVERS, WILLIAM.   op. 1779
This gentleman exhibited three works at the R.A. in 1779 of Dogs, A Leveret and Two Mice. He was an Honorary Exhibitor.

LEWIS, JOHN FREDERICK, R.A., R.W.S.   1805-1876
The eldest son of the engraver F. C. Lewis, he was 3 years younger than Landseer. As boys they used to go to sketch the lions kept at the Exeter Exchange. Lewis studied to be an engraver under his father and was only permitted to paint one day a week until, at 15, one of his paintings was well hung at the B.I.: thereafter he was allowed to become a painter. Initially he devoted himself to animal-painting with enough success to earn an adequate income. Early examples of his exhibits are 'Gamekeepers Deer Shooting' in 1824, 'A Group of His Majesty's Staghounds' in 1826, and two pictures of Hounds in 1829. He published a collection of etchings in 1825. Occasionally Lawrence employed him to paint the animals required in his portrait compositions – a common practice in those days. But he was destined for wider fields than those grazed by domestic animals. He turned from oils to watercolours and after a 2-year visit to Spain and Italy, his bold and richly coloured work earned him the soubriquet of 'Spanish' Lewis. In 1843 he went to Egypt and, using Cairo as his base, became enthralled by the Near East. He remained there for 8 years, his style becoming more detailed and his colours brighter.
In 1857 he was made President of the O.W.C.S. He became a full member of the R.A. in 1865.
Coll: Newcastle A.G.

LLOYD, EDWARD.   op. 1864-1891
This Shropshire man painted hunting scenes and animals. Portraits of 'Two Hunters and a Groom' and 2 harnessed coach horses with coachman and 'tiger' at Ellesmere are examples of his work. In 1861 he sent his only exhibit to the R.A. of Shropshire Down Sheep.

LODER, EDWIN.   op. 1840-1885
A son of James L., he too worked in Bath as a painter of animals, producing portraits of hunters, cattle, and dogs. A black greyhound in an open landscape dated 1885 is recorded.

LODER, JAMES.   op. 1820-1857   'of Bath'
This good provincial animal painter, who lived in Bath, first made his name locally by painting portraits of cattle for improver-breeders. He progressed to painting hunters, race-horses, and hunting groups, some of which were engraved. He became highly esteemed in the West Country but did not exhibit in London, so was not widely known in his lifetime.
In 1820 G. Hunt made an aquatint of his 'A Favourite Cob, harnessed'. In 1857 C. Hunt aquatinted a large print after his 'William Long on "Milkman" with hounds'.
Illustrated in B.S.P.
Coll: Exeter A.G.; Reading.

LODGE, GEORGE E.   1860-1954
From his youth he was a keen naturalist and falconer, becoming friends with J. G. Millais (q.v.) and A. Thorburn (q.v.). He studied and worked in London before moving to live at Camberley. Although primarily a painter and illustrator of birds – he illustrated Bannerman's 'Birds of the British Isles' – more rarely he used animals as his subjects. He wrote and illustrated 'Memoirs of an Artist Naturalist'.
He exhibited 7 works at R.A., and 3 at S.S.
Coll: Belfast.

LONGBOTTOM, ROBERT J.   op. 1830-1848
This landscape painter of Welsh scenes is better known for his portraits of horses and dogs, some of which were engraved by Greig, an example being his portrait of the greyhound 'Silverlocks'. Among his pictures exhibited at R.A. were, in 1830, a portrait of a 'Favourite Setter'; in 1831, 'Interior with Horses'; in 1832, 'Portrait of a Setter'; and in 1834 'A Study of Horses'.
He exhibited 10 works at R.A., 5 at B.I., 14 at S.S.

LUARD, LOWES DALBIAC. 1872-1944
This painter of horses for long worked in France. His sketches and illustrations of horses hauling heavy
loads were masterly. His deep scientific study of the horse resulted in the book 'The Horse: its Action and
Anatomy'. His memorial exhibition was held at the Birmingham A.G. in 1946, where an example of his
work is to be found.
He exhibited 4 works at R.A.

LUCAS LUCAS, H. F.   op. 1879-1926
This Rugby painter's career was spent in painting the portraits of hunters, usually in their stables.
Occasionally he was commissioned to paint a race-horse, such as 'Bard y Guary', second to 'Ormonde' in
the 1886 Derby.
Coll: Walker A.G.

LUKER, Wm., R.B.A.   op. 1849-1898
This Cheshire artist painted horses and equestrian groups among more general subjects.
He painted the race-horses 'Double Chance' and 'Security' with her foal. Among his R.A. Exhibits were
'Deer Stalkers with a Deer Hound and Pony' and a 'Retriever and Spaniels'.
He was the father of Wm. Luker, Jnr., b.1867, op. 1886-92.
He exhibited 57 works at R.A., 29 at B.I., 127 at S.S.

LUTYENS, Captain CHARLES HENRY AUGUSTUS. 1829-1915
This regular Army officer contributed several inventions to musketry before becoming a well-known painter
of portraits, hunters, and race-horses: one of this latter being 'Doncaster', the 1873 Derby winner.
The eleventh of his fourteen children became the famous architect, Sir Edwin Lutyens.
He exhibited 41 works at R.A., 11 at B.I., 1 at S.S.

LYNE, MICHAEL. 1912 - living artist
The son of a Herefordshire parson, he showed early promise as a sporting artist. He has painted many
sporting subjects and hunted his own pack of beagles. He has been commissioned to paint many famous
hunts, both here and in U.S.A., as well as portraits of race-horses. He has held his own exhibitions in
London. Examples of his work are in the Mellon Coll: and in Government Houses of Australia and New
Zealand.

LYON, DAVID. op. 1774
The work of this early artist is rare. 3 pictures are so far recorded from his hand. they are 'Dogs and Horses',
'A Huntsman on Horseback with his Hounds' and 'A Sportsman with Dog Coursing a Hare'.
He exhibited 2 works at F.S. in 1774.

MAGGS, JOHN CHARLES. 1819-1896
The son of James Maggs, a japanner of furniture, he was a native and resident of Bath where he ran a
painting school known as the Bath Art Studio. He achieved great popularity for his expert and accurate
scenes of driving and coaching – a nostalgic subject in the new age of steam. He was patronised by Royalty
and the nobility. He produced a series of famous coaching inns and another series of 80 metropolitan inns.
As well as coaching subjects, he painted views of Bath and its buildings and occasionally the portraits of
race-horses, such as 'Flying Dutchman', the Derby and St. Leger winner of 1849.
Illustration in B.S.P.

MAIDEN, JOSEPH. 1813-1843
The son of a coachman, coach-driver, and publican at Bury, an employer of his father sent him to Charles
Calvert (q.v.) at Manchester for instruction. He displayed considerable versatility, becoming best known for
his pictures of horses and dogs though his landscapes were highly esteemed. He first exhibited in 1832 at
the Royal Manchester Institute his 'Horses in a Thunderstorm'. In 1840 he showed there 'Alpine Mastiffs'
and in 1841 'The Bury Hunt'.
Charles Hunt aquatinted his portrait of the greyhound 'Sultan'.

MALBON, WILLIAM. op. 1834-1848
This Sheffield painter produced landscape, farmyard, and market scenes as well as occasionally painting

portraits of horses and dogs. He was in demand by fellow artists to insert human and animal figures in their landscapes.

He exhibited 1 sporting work at S.S. in 1834.

Coll: The Sheffield and Nottingham A.G's.

MALING, S.   op. 1726

A single work of this early artist is recorded. It is of a Huntsman with a Pack of Harriers with a village in the distance, signed and dated 1726.

MARKHAM, C.   op. 1851

A Chestnut racehorse with jockey up in a landscape dated 1851 by this painter is recorded.

MARSHALL, BENJAMIN.   1768-1835

One of the greatest of English sporting artists, second only to Stubbs, he was a native of Leicestershire. By 1791 he was working in London and received instruction in portraiture from a fellow-Leicestershire artist, Lemuel Francis Abbott.

It was said that Gilpin's 'Death of a Fox' exhibited at the R.A. in 1793 turned his attention to sporting subjects, chiefly racing and hunting scenes, although he had painted a portrait of the race-horse 'Escape' in 1792. In general the character studies of the humans in his pictures remain superior to those of his horses, which, whatever their colour, are too much alike; in this respect he is inferior to his pupil Ferneley, in capturing the individuality of a horse. It was fashion, however, that dictated the size of his figures' heads – in those days a thoroughbred's head had to seem small while the top-hat exaggerated that of its owner.

The first of 49 of his works was published in the Old Sporting Magazine in 1798. He did not exhibit at the R.A. until 1800 – and thereafter only intermittently – nor did he ever receive from it any recognition of his considerable talents. But these were widely recognised and he did not lack commissions.

From about 1804 he entered the second phase of his career: he became increasingly pre-occupied with the anatomy of his horses. Stubbs' great work on this subject had appeared in 1766. Marshall delighted to paint the play of light on their coats and the play of muscles beneath, with the greatest accuracy. In 1812 he went to live in Newmarket.

A severe coaching accident in 1819, from which he made a painful partial recovery, affected the rest of his career. Two years later the first of his articles on racing appeared in the Sporting Magazine under the pseudonym 'Observator' when he successfully described in words the scene which he could now paint with difficulty. He continued to paint and write until 1833 but his artistic powers never fully recovered. His work declined in popularity and he died poor.

He exhibited 13 works at R.A.

Coll: Royal Coll., the Tate Gal., the Mellon Coll., Leicester A.G.

Illustration in B.S.P.

MARSHALL, JOHN.   op. 1840-1896

This sporting painter exhibited at the R.A. of 1848 his portrait of the steeple-chaser 'The Curate'. He lived at Croydon and also painted genre, fruit, and still life. His son, J. Fitz Marshall, included animals in his range.

He exhibited 3 works at R.A., 17 at S.S.

MARSHALL, LAMBERT.   1810-1870

Born at Newmarket, the youngest son of the great Benjamin, he could not fail to be influenced by his father. At 16 his portrait of Ben was engraved by Fry for the Sporting Magazine of September 1826. Shaw Sparrow detected his father's hand in this and in the 25 other engravings from him of racehorses and sporting subjects published in it between 1826 and 1836. 'The Bull Ring Snug' of c.1840 is also recorded.

After this year his work was no longer recorded but he continued to paint until 1870.

MARSHALL, WILLIAM ELSTOB.   op. 1836-1881

An early work by this painter of genre was a portrait of a black and white Shetland pony.

He exhibited 8 at R.A., 5 at B.I., 18 at S.S.

MARTIN, SYLVESTER.   op. 1867-1906

This sporting painter of hunting scenes occasionally painted portraits of horses, such at 'Brighton', a steeple-chaser.

46

MATTHEWS, J. op. 1900's
A single example of work by this painter of the steeple-chaser 'King Harold', dated 1906, in a loose-box, does not indicate anything more than amateur skill.

MEARNS, A. op.1853-1864
This Lewisham artist painted dogs and sport. He showed at B.I. in 1853 'Pointers' and in 1856 'Clumber Spaniels'.
He exhibited 4 works at B.I., 2 at S.S.

MEASE, J. op. 1790-1810
Few examples of this artist's work are recorded. In 1790 he painted a White Terrier in a landscape; in 1797 he exhibited at the R.A. a Portrait of a Hunter and Portrait of Mr. Sheridan's horse, 'Billy'. Another picture, dated 1810, by his hand was of a Gentleman on his Hunter in a landscape with huntsmen and hounds.
He exhibited 2 works at R.A.

MEDLEY, SAMUEL. 1769-1857
This Liverpool-born artist was chiefly a painter of portraits and historical scenes. Pictures of animals were included in his œuvre.
He exhibited 2 works at R.A.

MEW, THOMAS HILLIER. op. 1850-1860
This Isle of Wight artist painted horse-portraits. One such of 'Thormanby', the 1860 Derby winner, is recorded. He was the brother of Frederick Mew, an architect.

MILLAIS, H. RAOUL. living artist
Grandson of Sir John Millais, P.R.A., he studied at Byam Shaw's under Vicat Cole and Ernest Jackson. His pen drawings, which have been compared with those of Constantine Guys, are often preliminary studies for small panels in oils. His subjects include racing and hunting scenes, equestrian portraits, and those of leading race-horses.

MILLAIS, JOHN GUILLE. 1865-1931
The 4th son of Sir John Millais, P.R.A., he was educated at Marlborough and Trinity, Cambridge, before serving in the Army for 11 years until 1893. During this time he travelled the world shooting big game; he was one of the first to study wild life in its natural habitat. He became an outstanding naturalist, as well as an artist, author, and animal sculptor, and counted George Lodge and Archibald Thorburn among his friends.
He illustrated many books on sport and Natural History. He was the author of about twenty books on subjects ranging from the Life of Selous to one on Magnolias.
Exhibitions of his paintings were held at the Fine Art Society in 1910 and 1921.

MILLNER, WILLIAM EDWARD. 1849-1895
This Lincolnshire painter of animals and genre was the son of William Millner, an artist and teacher. He was fond of painting horses under working conditions. Examples of his work are in the Museum at Gainsborough where he lived all his life.
His 'Wayside Gossip' of 1873 is in the Tate.

MONEY, KEITH. 1935 --living artist
This landscape and animal painter was born in New Zealand and now lives in Norfolk.
He first exhibited in London in 1961 and has recently completed a portrait of the race-horse 'Brigadier Gerard'.
He is the author of several books and is currently engaged on 'The Art of Alfred Munnings'.
Coll : Mellon.

MOODY, Miss FANNIE. 1861-*c*.1897
The daughter of F. W. Moody and pupil of J. T. Nettleship, she belonged to the Couldery class of painter

of domestic animals whose pictures are the delight of maiden ladies. Surprisingly, she was married (to Gilbert King) and knew Rossetti and his circle.

MORIER, DAVID.   1704-1770

A Swiss from Berne who came to England in 1743, he was another foreigner, like Wyck and Tillemans, who influenced our native school. Introduced to the Duke of Cumberland shortly after the Battle of Dettingen, he received royal patronage and a pension until the latter's death in 1765. He painted battle-scenes, equestrian portraits, dogs, and horses.

Young Sawrey Gilpin, who came into the Duke's employ in 1761, must have been familiar with his work and Stubbs seems to have been influenced by his portrait of the Godolphin Arabian.

Four years after his patron's death, Morier was in a debtor's prison, and when he died the Society of Artists met his funeral expenses.

Among his exhibits at the Society of Artists he showed in 1762 George II on Horseback and in 1768 'An Old Horse and the Farmer'.

Coll: Hull A.G.

MORLAND, GEORGE CHARLES.   1763-1804

Born in London, the son of the painter Henry Morland and his French wife, he showed early signs of genius. At 14 he was apprenticed to his father, to whose stern teaching some credit must be given for the technical mastery of his art that appeared a natural gift. His first painting was accepted by the R.A. in 1781. By 1786 when he married James Ward's sister, he had already made a reputation for his rustic genre subjects and scenes of childhood. To children he was devoted. After the arrival of a stillborn child in 1787 and the knowledge that his wife could bear no more, his weakness for drink took an ever-increasing hold on him and was to be the cause of his early death.

As an animal painter Morland, who affected to be 'horsey', was greatly influenced by Stubbs. The horses that he depicted with such realism were the equine equivalents to his rustic humans, rough and hard-working, and painted from accurate observation and a thorough knowledge of anatomy. Horses apart, he painted more pigs than any other animal with such success that he was dubbed a 'pig-painter'. His cows were those to be seen every day – quite unlike the bloated pedigree cattle – while his calves reveal his fondness for young creatures. His dogs show the same accuracy and careful observation with which he painted horses: whether mongrels or well-bred sporting dogs, he caught their own individuality.

Many of the estimated 3,000 of his paintings were engraved. As the effects of dissipation took hold, so the quality of his work deteriorated.

He exhibited 38 works at R.A., 33 at S.A., and 33 at F.S.

Coll: N.G., Tate, V. & A., Fitzwilliam, N.G. of Scotland, Glasgow, Nottingham, Birmingham, Birkenhead, Bournemouth, Hull, Leeds, Leicester, Newcastle A.G's, and the Mellon Coll.

MORLEY, GEORGE.   op. 1831-1873

This painter first gained recognition after receiving commissions from Princess Victoria and the Earls of Rosebery and Surrey, but his work is now rarely seen. He painted many chargers for officers, and dogs and horses for the Royal Family.

His exhibits at the R.A. in 1839 were a 'Stag at Bay', 2 portraits of Arab horses, and 2 horses belonging to the Queen.

He exhibited 40 works at R.A. and 2 at B.I., nearly all of horses and dogs.

MORLEY, ROBERT, R.B.A.   1857-1941

This artist, a pupil at the Slade under Poynter and Legros, studied further in Munich and Rome. After 1888 he turned from figure painting to landscape and animals. He became Hon. Secretary of R.S.B.A. in 1890.

He exhibited 5 at R.A., 30 at S.S.

Coll: Bristol.

MORRIS, ALFRED.   op. 1853-1873

This Deptford man painted animals, game, and sport. His R.A. exhibits were landscapes.

He showed 2 works at R.A., 17 at B.I., 14 at S.S.

MORRIS, JOHN C. op. 1851-1864

A pupil of Sydney Cooper, he painted landscape and animals, often on large canvasses, in Highland settings. His subjects were cattle, ponies, and dogs.

He lived in Greenwich and Deptford.

He exhibited 9 works at the R.A. (from 1851-63), 19 at B.I., and 16 at S.S.

Coll: Birmingham A.G.

MORRIS, W. WALKER. op. 1850-1867

This Victorian painted pictures of animals, chiefly dogs, in the style of Landseer and Ansdell. They were often in Highland settings and included dead game birds, competent enough of their kind and with more merit than some. His 'Gamekeeper's Son' was hung at the R.A. of 1856. It is assumed that he was the brother of John C. and Alfred Morris as they lived at the same address in Greenwich and Deptford.

He exhibited 7 works at R.A., 14 at B.I., 12 at S.S.

MOSELEY R. S. op. 1862-1893

He painted animals and genre.

He exhibited at the R.A., B.I. and S.S.

MUNNINGS, Sir ALFRED J., P.R.A. 1879-1959

Shortly after the end of his apprenticeship to a Norwich firm of lithographers in 1898, he started to exhibit at the R.A. pictures of East Anglian landscape and rural life, which included fairs, gypsies, cattle and ponies. In these he displayed, with the broad strong handling of his paint, an early command of colour and of the play of light and shade. Not so widely known as his later more 'finished' set paintings, they are of considerable merit.

It was not until 1919 that he received his first commission for an equestrian portrait and from then he went on to paint many famous race-horses, hunting groups, and racing scenes with a mastery that made him the outstanding animal painter of his day and the first ever to be made P.R.A. His 'Friesian Bull', a study in greens, can be compared with the best work of Paul Potter or James Ward. He published 2 volumes of autobiography. His widow founded a Museum devoted to his work at Dedham.

He exhibited 114 works at the R.A.

Hardly a museum of note does not possess an example of his work.

Illustration in B.S.P.

MURRAY, WILLIAM. op. 1800-1807

This Scottish artist painted small pictures of dogs and hounds.

McLEOD, JULIET. b.1917 - living artist

After studying in Paris she was apprenticed to Lynwood Palmer from 1933-1939. She has painted the portraits of many famous race-horses for British and foreign owners and has held exhibitions in London. She wrote and illustrated 'A Hundred Horses', published in 1960.

Illustration in B.S.P.

NEALE, EDWARD. op. 1850-1910

This ornithologist and artist painted the wild birds and animals of the Scottish countryside.

He exhibited 1 work at R.A., 6 at BI., 9 at S.S.

Illustration in B.S.P.

NEDHAM, WILLIAM. op. 1823-1849

Guy Paget thought that this painter was a Leicestershire amateur from Syston and that he was a pupil of Ferneley.

His picture of Dick Burton, a famous hunt servant in the Shires, is dated 1826. The wooden handling of the hounds in this smacks of an amateur. Another picture, dated 1823, was of Mr. Pochin's 'Favourite Hunter with Groom'. 'A Huntsman on a Bay Hunter with Hounds' before a Country House by Nedham dated 1849 passed recently through the sale-rooms.

Coll: Leicester A.G., 'Horse and Rider' d.1836.

NETTLESHIP, JOHN TRIVETT. 1841-1902

Born in Kettering, after schooling in Durham he entered his father's solicitor's office. From there he went to

Heatherley's and the Slade. He studied at the Zoo to become an animal painter. He started exhibiting at the R.A. in 1871. He visited India and painted a Chetah hunt. He worked as an illustrator and was the author of two books on Browning's Poetry and George Morland's Influence. He worked in pastel in later life and sometimes drew the animals in other artists' pictures. His daughter was married to Augustus John. He exhibited 20 works at R.A., 1 at S.S., and 3 at N.W.C.S.

NEWCOMEN, Mrs. OLIVE.   op. 1866-1870
This lady exhibited at the B.I. in 1866 a 'Sheep Dog' and in 1867 'Loading a Cart'. In 1866 she showed at the R.A. a 'Clumber Spaniel's Head and a Teal' and in after years two picures of cart-horses.

NEWMARSH, G. B.   op. c. 1828-1849
In 1828 Pyall aquatinted his picture of the race-horse 'Sharper'. A Groom leading a bay hunter and a picture of prize cattle near Birmingham are recorded.

NIGHTINGALE, BASIL.   1864-1940
The youngest son of Robert, and the only one to follow him, he lived in Dorset, Somerset, and Warwickshire, painting sporting scenes and portraits of horses. He worked in oils, pastel, and pencil. He painted 'Ormonde', the Triple Crown winner of 1886 and 'Bendigo'. In his picture of Gillard, huntsman of the Belvoir for 27 years, blowing hounds away at the gallop, horse and hounds were portraits

*NIGHTINGALE, ROBERT.   1815-1895
This artist lived at Maldon, Essex, where he was apprenticed to J. Stannard before entering the R.A. Schools in 1837.
He painted portraits, fruit, and landscape as well as sporting scenes and portraits of horses. For 20 years he was commissioned by the vast Lord Chaplin to paint portraits of his hunters which speaks well for his ability to 'get' a likeness.
He exhibited 4 works at R.A. and 25 at S.S.

NOBLE, JOHN SARGEANT, R.B.A.   1848-1896
This pupil of Landseer first studied in the R.A. Schools. His most frequent subjects were gun-dogs, often in Highland settings, and otter-hounds and otter-hunting.
Shaw Sparrow saw him as a 'hyphen-painter' who made a connection between his fore-runners and more modern styles. His straight forward well-painted work is still of more appeal to sportsmen than to connoisseurs. He painted in watercolour less frequently than in oils.
He exhibited in London from 1866 and became R.B.A. the following year.
He showed 46 works at R.A. and 96 at S.S.
Coll: The V. & A., Leeds and Birmingham A.G's.

NODDER, R. P.   op. 1786-1820
The work of this painter of animals and birds is scarce but worthy of note. His early exhibits were mostly portraits of dogs: later he showed some of horses, which were followed by a series of bird studies. He worked in London.
References to him were made in the Sporting Magazine.
His brother, F. P. Nodder, was appointed Botanical Painter to George III.
He exhibited 27 works at R.A.
Illustration in B.S.P.

*NORTHCOTE, JAMES, R.A.   1746-1831
This Plymouth-born pupil of Joshua Reynolds made his name as a portrait and historical subject painter. But he produced so many fine paintings of both domestic and wild animals that he cannot be ommitted from this voluume. Among his many exhibits at the R.A. he showed in 1797 'Leopards'; in 1798 'Two Monkeys'; in 1804 'Tiger Hunting'; in 1817 a 'Tiger's Den'. At the B.I. he showed in 1808 'A Dog and a Hawk'. in 1831 'A Lion at Rest'. His Sportsman's Dog' was mezzotinted in 1800 by S. W. Reynolds, who also engraved in colours his 'Leopards'.
He exhibited 229 works at R.A., 22 at B.I., 15 at S.S.

*NORTON, BENJAMIN CAM.   op. 1862-1890
This Sheffield landscape artist painted portraits of hunters and race-horses with superior skill. As these were

privately commissioned he did not exhibit, so that only recently has his work become more widely known. As well as favourite hunters in loose-boxes, he painted race-horses with their jockeys in landscape and race-course settings. Such was his 'Fortissimo', winner of the Goodwood Stakes of 1882 with G. Fordham up. He worked at Newmarket.

He exhibited 2 works at the B.I. in 1862.

NOVICE, WILLIAM. op. 1809-1813
In 1809 he showed at the R.A. the interior of a Smith's shop and the next year a large Blacksmith's Shop at the B.I., to which later he sent a few pictures of games of draughts.

His portrait of Tom Oldaker, the Old Berkeley huntsman, riding with his hounds, was dated 1813.

He was the father of George W. and W. F. Novice.

NOVICE, W. F. op. 1828-1829
Sharing the same house in London as his brother George W., in 1828 he sent to the R.A. 'Dog's Head from Nature' to be followed next year by 'Study of a Dog's Head'. After this the career of Novice and his dog lapsed into obscurity.

OLDMEADOW, F. A. op. 1840-1866
This painter, who lived in Bushey, was commissioned by the Marquis of Westminster and exhibited at the R.A. portraits of 'Touchstone' in 1840 and of his broodmares 'Banter' and 'Maid of Honour' in 1841. In 1844 he showed 'An Arabian and his Horse' and in 1847 Mr. Preston's steeple-chaser 'Brunette'. His work appears rarely.

He exhibited 6 works at R.A.

OSBORNE, WILLIAM, R.H.A. 1823-1901
This Irishman painted portraits and animals. He was the father of W. E. Osborne, portrait and landscape painter. He was a student at R.H.A., Dublin, where he mostly exhibited. Many of his pictures are of dogs and hunting groups.

OVEREND, WILLIAM. op. 1845-1855
This painter portrayed the race-horse 'Dandy Jim' at Doncaster. Perhaps he was the father of William Heysham Overend (1851-1898), the marine painter.

PAICE, GEORGE. op. 1878-1924
This unimportant painter produced landscapes and portraits of hunters in their boxes and of dogs. An example was of the race-horse 'Maidstone Masher' with a collie in a landscape. He lived at Croydon. He painted 'Sansovino', Derby winner of 1924.

He exhibited 6 works at the R.A. from 1887-97 and 4 at S.S.

Coll: Leeds A.G.

PAGE, HENRY MAURICE. op. 1878-1890
This landscape artist painted animals and sporting moorland scenes. He lived in London and Croydon.

He exhibited 11 works at R.A. and 54 at S.S.

PALFREY, PENRY POWELL. 1830-1902
Born and brought up in London, though of Welsh extraction, he was employed commercially designing and executing work in stone, stained glass, church decoration, and heraldic subjects. He spent his leisure painting horses, but did not become a full-time painter of these until 1884 when he was encouraged to do so by the Duke of Westminster. He came to the notice of Queen Victoria in 1886 and was given commissions by her. His studies of horses in watercolour are finely observed and executed. It was not until 1894 that he came to full flower in the painting of coaching scenes. He illustrated books written by his friend and patron, Sir Walter Gilbey, who reckoned that he was one of the best animal painters of his period.

His work remains relatively unknown.

PALMER, LYNWOOD. 1868-1939
As a young man this son of a Canon emigrated to Canada and worked on a ranch. When his talent for drawing horses became recognised, he moved to New York, returning to England after an absence of 11 years.

He was commissioned to paint Edward VII's Derby winner 'Minoru' and George V's 'Scuttle' and 'Limelight' and many other winners of the Classics. His friendship with Algenon Talmadge, R.A., had a beneficial effect on his art. He excelled at getting the likeness of a race-horse, being able even to show its state of training, taking immense pains with sketches, photographs, and the tape measure to achieve his results. He received high prices for his commissions.

Coll: Belfast Museum, Doncaster A.G.

Illustration in B.S.P.

PANT, T.   op. 1813

A portrait by this painter of a Prize Bull in a barn, signed and dated 1813, is recorded.

PARK, HENRY.   1816-1871

Born in Bath, he studied at the Royal Academy Schools and returned west to live in Bristol where he gained a reputation as a painter of animals and landscape. 'A Summer Afternoon' dated 1854, is a competently painted scene showing cattle and horses round a pond.

He exhibited 4 works each at the R.A. and S.S. and 1 at the B.I.

Illustration in B.S.P.

PASMORE, JOHN.   op. 1830-1845

He painted animals, birds, and sporting scenes.

He exhibited 11 at R.A., 3 at B.I., 3 at S.S.

PASMORE, J. F.   op. 1838-1881

It is not known what relation he was to the above. In addition to portraits of dogs and ponies, he painted fish, still life, and rural genre.

He exhibited 30 works at R.A., 23 at B.I., and 11 at S.S.

PATON, FRANK.   1856-1909

This illustrator worked in London and Gravesend, painting genre and animals in oils and watercolour. His subjects ranged from pictures of wild rabbits and dogs retrieving game to a portrait of the unbeaten 'Ormonde', winner of the Two Thousand Guineas, Derby, and St. Leger of 1886.

He exhibited 20 works at the R.A. from 1878-90, and 4 at S.S.

PAUL, Sir JOHN DEAN.   1775-1852

A Banker and Melton hunting man, he was an amateur artist of superior talent. Perhaps best known for his 'Trip to Melton Mowbray', a set of 14 prints in scroll form, he painted many hunting scenes and portraits of horses as well as landscape. His set of the 'Leicestershire Hunt', entitled 'Gaudet Equis Canibusque' was engraved.

He exhibited 20 works at R.A., 1802-1837.

Coll: Leicester A.G.

PAYNE, CHARLES J.   1884-1967   'Snaffles'

Reproductions of the work of this sporting artist who painted much in watercolour remain extremely popular. He produced many books, illustrating with humour, scenes of hunting, racing, and pig-sticking. Strictly, he was more a sporting than an animal painter.

PEARCE, STEPHEN.   1819-1904

The father of this equestrian portrait and animal painter was a clerk in the department of the Master of Horse, so being reared in the Royal Mews gave him unlimited opportunity to study horses. His training continued at Sass' Academy, and the R.A. Schools; he became a pupil of Archer Shee who had been made P.R.A. in 1830.

His first exhibits sent to the R.A. were portraits of horses in the Royal Stables but he extended his scope to become a successful and prolific painter of equestrian portrait groups in pleasant landscape settings. In an age when presentation pictures were in high fashion these commissions, and the plates reproduced from them, were very lucrative. His style, which had been hard and tight, gradually became freer as his career progressed.

A year before he died he published a book of memoirs illustrated by 19 of his pictures and including a list of his works.
He exhibited 92 works at R.A. and 3 at B.I.
Illustration in B.S.P.

PENNESTONE, H.   op. 1848
This Rutland primitive painted the portrait of an immense ox at Oakham in 1848.

PERRY, G.   op. 1831
A well-painted portrait of a Chestnut race-horse, with jockey up, in a race-course setting, dated 1831 and signed, is recorded.
It is not known if he was related to Alfred Perry, the landscape painter, who occasionally painted portraits of animals.

*PHYSICK, ROBERT, R.B.A.   op. 1859-1866
This little-known animal painter exhibited 5 works at the R.A. from 1859-64; 4 at the B.I., and 18 at S.S.
It is not known how he was related to T. Physick, op. 1847-72, who came from Lancaster and painted continental scenes.

PITMAN, JOHN.   op. 1820-1842
This Worcestershire man painted portraits of cattle and horses. Hullmandel engraved his 'Madresfield Heifer'. A 'Cattle and Dog in a Landscape' of 1836 is recorded.

POLLARD, JAMES.   1792-1867
The son of Robert Pollard, painter, engraver, and publisher of prints, he was London-born. He received encouragement from Thomas Bewick and strove with success to become the leading illustrator and recorder of coaching scenes and coaches in their heyday, as well as producing pictures and engravings of all kinds of sport. He must be regarded as an artist of these rather than an animal painter, though he painted portraits of animals occasionally. An example is his picture of the race-horse 'Cotherston'.
Coll: The Mellon Coll. and Walker A.G.
Lit. 'James Pollard – Painter of the Age of Coaching' (1965)   'The Golden Age of Coaching & Sport' (1972) both by W. C. Selway.
He exhibited 5 works at R.A., 3 at B.I., 4 at S.S.

PONSONBY, SARAH.   1943 - living artist
This artist studied in Florence and Milan. She paints horses, dogs, and racing scenes and is also a Sculptress. She has exhibited in London since 1967 at the Tryon Gallery.

PRINGLE, Wm.   op. 1840-1858
This painter of horses and sporting scenes is thought to have lived in Birmingham. His portrait of Mr. Sprigge's bay mare 'Chance' with jockey up in a landscape setting is well painted. Pavière in B.S.P. records his Stourbridge-Birmingham Mail passing Quinton Toll Gate of 1842.
He exhibited 1 work at B.I., 3 at S.S.

PYBOURNE, THOMAS.   b. 1708 - op. 1734
This early horse-painter is known for his portrait of 'Flying Childers' being brought to be watered – a setting similar to that used by Wootton several times, which might indicate that he was a pupil or assistant to the Master. Another signed work shows more talent than this conventional portrait: it is of 2 race-horses being rubbed down by strappers, one of whom has been kicked sprawling to the ground. It shows vigour and observation in its execution.
His portrait of a race-horse with jockey in bright cerise colours further indicates a connection with Wootton, the background being peopled with galloping horsemen on Newmarket Heath.

QUADAL, MARTIN FERDINAND.   op. 1772-d.1811
This Moravian travelled to Ireland by way of Vienna and Russia. He became an instructor at the Hibernian Academy.
Painting portraits, military reviews, interiors of cottages, and stables, he became best known for his animal pictures. He also etched. He moved to London before returning to die in St. Petersburgh.

His first exhibit at the R.A. was in 1772, followed the next year by a picture of the King reviewing the Artillery and one of 'Dogs attacking a Tiger'. In 1793 he sent 'A Boy with a Dog and a Horse'.

QUIQLEY, D.   op. 1750-1773

More is known of this 18th century painter's subjects than about himself. He may have been an assistant to Seymour. He painted the famous 'Carriage Match at Newmarket' which was run in August 1750 and which Seymour painted for the Duke of Queensberry, in whose collection it remained until 1897. But Sir Joshua Reynolds owned a repetition of it, presumed to be from Seymour's hand.

Quiqley is known to have worked in Dublin, and in 1764 painted the 'Curragh of Kildare Races'. He also painted the 'Godolphin Arabian'. This outstanding stallion was imported as a 5-year old in 1729 and died in 1753. Only Wootton is recorded as having painted him from life, as a 7-year old. Such was his fame, however, that in due course Morier, Stubbs, James Roberts, and Quigley all produced their versions of his likeness.

QUINTON, J.   op. 1853-1884

Work by this painter is rare. A ploughman and his team returning home, portraits of a bay stallion in his box and of a saddled hunter with 2 dogs are recorded.

It is presumed that he was related to A. R. Quinton, the landscape painter.

RADDCLIFFE, J.   op. 1842

A picture signed and dated by him is recorded of Lord Jersey's 'Bay Middleton', winner of the 2,000 Gns. and Derby of 1836.

Named after the famous Leicestershire hunting character, this horse sired 2 Derby winners, The Flying Dutchman and Andover, so is regarded by some as of more interest than the artist.

RAVEN, SAMUEL.   1775-1847

This Birmingham artist painted sporting scenes on small panels and on the lids of boxes. A picture of Old English Sporting Dogs of fine quality is recorded. He should not be confused with John Samuel Raven, 1829-77.

READ, JOHN R.   op. 1773-1798

This Bedford artist was a painter of portraits, animals, flowers, birds, and a few landscapes. He became well-known for his paintings of dogs.

He exhibited 2 pictures of dead game at the R.A. in 1779 and 31 other works at S.A.

Illustration in B.S.P.

REINAGLE, PHILIP, R.A.   1749-1834

A pupil of Allan Ramsey, he was of Hungarian extraction. He came to London from Scotland in 1769 and completed his training in the R.A. Schools. From painting portraits he turned to painting, in a bold and masterly manner, birds, dogs, horses, and hunting scenes. But about 1794 he became more interested in landscape painting, which he executed in a rich and mellow style of the period. Sawrey Gilpin is known to have collaborated with him in painting the horses in some of his landscapes.

His 'Sportsman's Cabinet', a series of sporting dogs, was engraved by Scott.

Coll: V. & A., the Fitzwilliam, Sheffield and Wolverhampton A.G's.

He exhibited 114 works at R.A., 138 at B.I., and 1 at S.S.

Illustration in B.S.P.

REINAGLE, P. A.   op. 1804-1811

Headed by Philip, there were 12 artist members of this family. Of these, only one other P.A., can be considered as an animal painter, the prolific R.R., although painting many sporting scenes, being primarily a landscape artist.

P. A. Reinagle exhibited, in the course of 7 years, 8 portraits of horses, 4 at the R.A. and 4 at B.I.

RICHARDS, CHARLES.   op. 1854-1857

This Keynsham artist painted animals, sport, and rural genre. An R.A. exhibit was a 'Study of Sheep and Lambs'.

He exhibited 4 works at R.A., 4 at B.I., and 7 at S.S.

RIVIERE, BRITON, R.A. 1840-1920

Educated at Cheltenham College, where his father William was drawing master, he was a pupil of J. Pettie and W. Orchardson. He acquired a sound knowledge of anatomy, helped by his studies of animals at the Zoo, where, like many of his contemporaries, he became fascinated by the lions. He usually introduced animals in his historical and genre pictures.

He gained popularity from the engravings of his humorous, but sentimental, pictures of dogs.

His 1894 R.A. exhibit 'Beyond Man's Footsteps' was bought by the Chantrey Bequest.

Coll: The V. & A., Exeter, Whitworth A.G's.

ROBERTS, JAMES. c.1708-c.1760

He was an early draughtsman who worked in close conjunction with his brother Henry, an engraver. They published the portraits of about 40 well-known horses c. 1755.

Baldwyn published c.1760 the 'Sportsman's Pocket Companion' with illustrations drawn by James and engraved by Henry Roberts.

ROBERTS, Samuel. op 1778-1782

Of minor interest, this early artist showed 4 pictures at the R.A. The subjects were hares, fish, and mallard.

ROE, ROBERT HENRY. 1793-1880

This painter of Scottish Highland sporting scenes, including animals and birds, later worked in London and Cambridge where he was connected with an art business.

His 1853 R.A. exhibit was 'The Tired Stag'.

He was father of Frederick, historical and watercolour painter, of Clarence, who produced similar Scottish work of stags and deer, and of Colin Graeme (q.v.).

He exhibited 10 works at R.A., 11 at B.I., and 16 at S.S.

ROPER, RICHARD. c.1730-1775

One of the early animal-painters of the school of Wootton, his horses are less stereotyped than those of some of his contemporaries and his back-grounds more varied.

His work should be distinguished from that of Thomas Roper, an artist of inferior talent.

He exhibited 9 works at the Free Society, and 3 at Society of Artists.

Illustration in B.S.P.

ROSA, GWILYM. op. 1856-1872

Little is known of this Welsh painter. His portrait of Charles Davis, huntsman of the Royal Buckhounds (and brother of R. B. Davis), is dated 1856. His portrait group of five hounds of the now extinct Vale of Ayon Hunt in a landscape setting, is dated 1872.

He did not exhibit in London.

ROSS, JAMES. op. 1729-1733

A family of this name who lived near Gloucester has caused confusion of identity. It is believed that James was the brother of Thomas, op. 1730-1745, an early and accomplished landscape artist.

The signed work of James shows that he was no humble provincial horse-painter. His large canvasses, usually of hunting scenes, are well composed with the figures placed in well-painted landscapes.

Shaw Sparrow considered that his four pictures of the Beaufort Hunt, dated 1729-31, were youthful in style and showed Wootton's influence.

'The Kill', dated 1732, of a hunt in a Somerset setting, is more mature, and as his work emerges from private sources his stature grows. A picture of a 'Hunt in Full Cry', dated 1733, is illustrated in B.S.P.

A James Ross engraved several views of the town of Hereford in 1778 from drawings by G. Powle but it is not certain that he was the same artist.

Illustration in B.S.P.

RUGGLES, WILLIAM H. op. 1833-1846

This Lewisham man painted portraits of people and of animals. A Greyhound in a Landscape of 1837 is recorded. His R.A. exhibit of 1846 was 'A Favourite Hunting Mare'.

He exhibited at the R.A. one portrait of a man and one of a horse.

RYMAN, E. V.
An undated signed portrait of a bay hunter held by a red-coated groom in a landscape setting is recorded.

RYOTT, J. R.   *c.* 1810-*c.*1860
This pre-Victorian, who worked at Newcastle, painted horses and sport. A set of four hunting scenes dated 1848 is recorded.

SANDBY, PAUL, R.A.   1725-1809
Sandby, who came from Nottingham, was appointed to the Military Drawing Office in London in 1741 and, after the Rebellion of 1745, worked as a draughtsman on the Military Survey of Scotland. In 1752 he went to live with his brother, Thomas, who was Deputy Ranger of Windsor Great Park under the Duke of Cumberland.
Called the 'Father of Water Colour', being the first to use it as paint and not merely to colour mono-chromes, his fame rests as a painter of landscape in that medium and in gouache. He was the first to paint real views from Nature and to popularize the beauties of the countryside. He reproduced the best of his work by his own improved process of aquatinting. Nor must be overlooked his clear and accurate drawings of humans and animals. Many of these, showing the Duke of Cumberland's servants and horses, are in the Royal Collection.
In 1768 he was appointed Chief Drawing Master at the Woolwich Royal Military Academy. He was a founder member of the R.A. Geo. III made him drawing master to his sons.
He exhibited 125 works at R.A., 39 at S.A., 14 at B.I., 2 at F.S.

SANDS, B.   op. 1859-1863
The work of this horse-painter is rarely seen. Usually he painted hunters in their loose-boxes: it is assumed that these pictures remain in private ownership.
He did not exhibit.

SANDYS-LUMSDANE, LEESA.   1936 - living artist
This artist spent her childhood in India, and on her return, studied at the Gloucester College of Art.
Her subjects are hunting and racing scenes as well as portraits of horses.
She has been exhibiting in London since 1967 at the Tryon Gallery.

SARTORIUS, FRANCIS.   1734-1804
The son of John N. Sartorius, Senior, who was his instructor in art, he carried on his father's primitive style of painting portraits of horses and hunting groups, fortunate that this was then in vogue. He might well be taken as a contemporary of James Seymour, his elder by 32 years, than of Stubbs, 10 years his senior, or Gilpin, 1 year older than he. He painted many hunting scenes set in washy landscape backgrounds, their foregrounds characterised by the insertion of foxhounds the size of beagles.
The appealing naivety of the work of the father seems archaic in that of the son.
He exhibited 12 at R.A., 20 at F.S., and 7 at S.A.
Illustration in B.S.P.

SARTORIUS (G) Wm.   *c.*1773-1789
A still life of strawberries and other soft fruit is recorded as well as an immature portrait of a greyhound bitch in an open landscape.
Perhaps he was the same man as G. W. Sartorius who showed a Fruit Piece at Free Society in 1773, some portraits of women in 1778 and 1779, and painted in 1785 a saddled bay hunter hitched to a tree in a landscape.
It is not known how he fitted on the family tree.

SARTORIUS, JOHN FRANCIS.   ?1775-1831
The eldest son of John N. Snr., he painted with less success though in the same style as other members of his family. In 1801 he exhibited at R.A. 'Racehorses going to the Start' and 'Racehorses Running' and in 1806 'Coursing at Hatfield Park', with portraits of the horses of the Marchioness of Salisbury. Scott engraved several plates from his designs for the Sporting Magazine, but as his father's work was still being published, they are hard to distinguish.
His pictures of sporting dogs and of dead game were done with meticulous care.

56

He exhibited 20 works at R.A., and 4 at S.S.

Illustration in B.S.P.

SARTORIUS, JOHN N., Snr.   1700-1780

The son of an engraver of Nuremburg, where he was born, by 1723 he was painting horse portraits in England. Shaw Sparrow called him an amateur who worked for a living but who remained an amateur for life. His 'primitive' portraits of race-horses are of more historical than artistic value, like the work of many of his contemporaries.

He exhibited 1 work at R.A., 1 at S.A., and 62 at F.S.

SARTORIUS, JOHN N., Jnr.   1759-1828

The well-known son of the much-married Francis, he was called 'Junior' to distinguish him from his grandfather John. He became the most famous of his family of sporting and animal painters. He was patronised by the leading sportsmen of the day, painting portraits of 'Escape' for the Prince of Wales, of 'Grey Diomed', of 'Phenomena', the Champion trotter, and of 'Eclipse' from the drawings of his father, as well as innumerable sporting scenes. At the start of his career, he worked in the primitive style of his father but gradually drew away from this, placing his figures in better composed and painted landscape settings. The Sporting Magazine published plates from his work engraved by Walker, Webb, and others from 1795-1827.

He exhibited 78 works at R.A., 31 at F.S., 1 at S.A.

Illustration in B.S.P.

Coll: Walker A.G.

SCANLAN, ROBERT R.   op. 1837-1859.   d.1876

This Irishman painted portraits, animals, and some historical subjects. He started exhibiting at R.A. in 1837, showing portraits of Lord Mount Charles and his pony and of two State Horses. Other later horse portraits shown were of the steeple-chaser 'Lottery' and of 'The Poacher'.

A pair of Horse-dealing aquatints after him by J. Harris was published in 1841.

SCHEICKHARDT, HEINRICH WILHELM.   1746-1797

A Prussian from Brandenburg who took refuge in England in 1786 shortly after being appointed Director of the Academy at the Hague, he was befriended by Benjamin West, P.R.A. In 1788 he dedicated to him a series of etchings of animals, for which he rates a mention in this volume.

Primarily a landscape artist, he specialised in paintings of snow and frost.

He exhibited 6 works at S.A., and 22 at B.I.

SCHWANFELDER, CHARLES HENRY.   1773-1837

This Leeds-born artist was a true Yorkshireman in all but his German name, practising mainly in that county and visiting London only occasionally. His range was wide, including portraits, animals, sporting scenes, and landscape – the last of excellent quality whether by itself or as a setting to his well-executed figures. Although he exhibited more in Yorkshire than London, his talents were appreciated there and he was appointed Animal Painter to the Prince Regent in 1816 and re-appointed in 1821 when the Regent became King.

Shaw Sparrow saw him as a link between the age of Stubbs and the Landseer-Herring era which benefited from his influence. The quality of his work puts him high in the ranks of provincial animal painters of his period.

He exhibited 10 works at R.A. and 6 at B.I. from 1809-1835.

Coll: Leeds and Nottingham A.G's.

SEAGO, EDWARD BRYAN.   b.1910 - living artist

This Norwich-born landscape artist and animal painter has exhibited at the R.A. since 1930 and held his own exhibitions in London. He has written and illustrated many books.

His animal portraits include the race-horses 'Fox Hunter', winner of the 1931 Gold Cup, and 'Alcester', while his equestrian groups include Lord Melchett, M.F.H., with Fred Napper and the Tedworth Hounds.

SEALY, ALLEN CULPEPER.   op. 1873-1899

This Londoner painted landscape, genre, horses and hunting scenes. Four plates of the last were reproduced in the Badminton Library volume on hunting.

His exhibits at the R.A. from 1875-1888 were landscapes. He exhibited also at S.S. A Race-horse and trainer in a landscape is dated 1899.
He exhibited 19 works at R.A., 21 at S.S.

SELFE, MADELEINE.   living artist
This artist, born at Sharnbrook, Beds., was trained for a musical career but with encouragement from Munnings and professional advice from Henry Lamb, she developed her talents as a painter of horses.
She now receives many commissions to paint blood-stock, steeple-chasers, and show jumpers. Her work is well known in this country and America.

SEXTIE, WILLIAM A.   op. 1848-1887
He lived at Marlborough and specialised in painting the portraits of race-horses. This he did in an exact and anatomically correct manner, but of Art there is little evidence, so his work is chiefly of historical value to bloodstock enthusiasts.
One of his last works was his portrait of 'St. Blaise', winner of the 1883 Derby.
He exhibited a picture of Lord Granville's favourite hack at the R.A. in 1848.

SEYMOUR, JAMES.   1702-1752
The son of a banker who was a friend of Lely and Wren, he gained contemporary fame as a painter of horses and of racing and hunting scenes, though apparently he had no formal training in art. He possessed, however, the ability of being able to observe and to draw.
Walpole says that he was thought superior to Wootton in drawing a horse but was too idle to apply himself to his profession. His popularity came from his genius for expressing on paper or canvas the individual characteristics and 'personality' of his horse subjects. Though often hard and stiff in technique, his pictures have vitality and great accuracy of detail – his grooms and huntsmen are real people in their 18th century setting.
Compared artistically to that of Wootton, his work is 'amateurish' but he remains the great 'primitive', relatively more popular and valued today than in his own age.
Illustration in B.S.P.
Coll: The Tate and Fitzwilliam.

SHAW, JOSHUA.   1776-1860
Born at Bellingborough, Lincs., he was apprenticed to a signwriter. Later he moved to Stockport and to Bath before going to London in 1813. Primarily a landscape painter, he painted flowers, still life, and animals; many of his landscapes included cattle that were finely and delicately painted.
This unusual man, who produced many a spurious Berchem and Du Jarden, emigrated in 1817 to America where he diverted himself from painting by inventing improvements to fire-arms that were taken up by the country of his adoption and by Russia.
He exhibited 9 works at R.A., 22 at B.I., and 2 at S.S.
Coll: V. & A., and Holburne Museum, Bath.

SHAW, WILLIAM JAMES, F.S.A.   op. 1757-1774
This old painter of horses was of the school of Wootton and until recently much of his work had sunk into obscurity. Shaw Sparrow found him uncouth in his early pictures but by 1757 when R. Houston published a popular mezzotint after him of Blank, son of the Godolphin Arabian, his technique had improved considerably; although the background was a standard one that appears with variations in at least 3 of Wootton's pieces. Grant considered his work showed more vivacity and action than that of his contemporaries. With success he built a specially fitted-up studio off Cavendish Square large enough to take his equine subjects.
He became a fellow of the Society of Artists.
He exhibited 27 works at S.A.

SHAYER, WILLIAM, R.B.A.   1788-1879
This long-lived and ever-popular artist was born and lived in Southampton, making the surrounding countryside, shores, and the New Forest the settings of his numberless landscapes. Self-taught, he painted these in an individual style, his colouring bright and clear, the figures usually groups of rustics or gypsies

with their animals – sheep, horses, and cattle. Well-painted though these latter were, he does not appear to have accepted commissions to paint portraits of any animals.

He exhibited 6 works at R.A., 82 at B.I., and 338 at S.S.

Coll: V. & A., Guildhall, Glasgow, Wolverhampton, Leicester, Bristol, and Southampton A.G's.

SHAYER, WILLIAM J.   1811-1867

One of the sons of William Shayer, he painted similar subjects in a manner so like his father's that his work can be mistaken despite its lack of fine colouring. Although his talents were inferior, his range was wider than his father's. It included farmyard, coaching, and hunting scenes as well as portraits of horses and dogs. His portrait of a famous American trotter 'Confidence' in a trotting race was painted in 1840. He painted 'Achievement', winner of the 1867 1,000 Gns., St. Leger, Coronation, and Doncaster Cups.

He exhibited 2 works at R.A., 1 at B.I., and 19 at S.S.

Coll: Glasgow A.G.

*SHEPHERD, DAVID.   1931 - living artist

After leaving school at Stowe, in 1949, he went to Kenya where his interest in wild life was aroused. On his return he studied painting for 2 years under Robin Goodwin, the marine and portrait painter. He first made his name painting aircraft for the R.A.F. In the course of this work he revisited Africa where he started painting its varied fauna with continuing success.

He held his first exhibition in London in 1962.

Coll: Belfast A.G.

SHERRIFF, JOHN, A.R.S.A.   1816-1844

The work of this short-lived Scottish artist is rare. His portrait of a famous greyhound 'Mountain Dew' with a game-keeper, dated 1839, shows a good knowledge of anatomy and composition: it must be regretted that he did not live long enough to fulfill its promise.

He exhibited at the R.S.A.

SHIELS, WILLIAM, R.S.A.   1785-1857

This Berwickshire-born artist painted rural genre, animals, and some mythological subjects, of which 'Ulysses and Lærtes, shown at R.A. in 1808, was an example.

His animals were set in well-painted, often Highland, surroundings. He was a founder member of the Scottish Academy in 1826, where he mostly exhibited.

He sent 8 works to R.A., 17 to B.I., 12 to S.S.

SILLEM, CHARLES.   op. 1883-1889

This little-known painter exhibited 'Rough Terrier and Rats' at the R.A. in 1883.

He sent 3 works to R.A. and 3 to S.S.

SIMPSON, CHARLES WALTER, R.I., R.O.I.   1885-1971

This painter of famous horses and their riders, of birds, and of sport, was born at Camberley, the son of a General. He won a Silver Medal in 1923 at the Paris Salon and Gold Medals at the San Francisco International Exhibition of 1914 and the VIII Olympiad at Paris in 1924.

An R.A. exhibition of his work was sent on tour of Municipal Galleries in 1956-58. He worked in oils, watercolours, and tempera.

Among books that he had published are 'Leicestershire and its Hunts', 'The Harboro' Country', 'Animal and Bird Painting', and 'The Fields of Home'.

Coll: V. & A., Derby, Doncaster, Newcastle, Plymouth, Sheffield and Bournemouth A.G's.

Illustration in B.S.P.

SKEAPING, JOHN R., R.A.   1901 - living artist

This eminent living painter and sculptor was born in Liverpool and was a pupil at the R.A. Schools. He was a Gold Medalist in 1920 and won the Prix de Rome in 1924.

He started exhibiting figures and landscapes at the R.A. in 1922 but turned more and more to horses and sporting subjects as his career advanced.

He was Professor of Sculpture, Royal College of Arts, from 1953-1959. He was advanced to full R.A. in 1959.

His publications include 'Animal Drawing' in 1934, 'How to Draw Horses' in 1938, and 'Les Animaux dans l'Art' (Paris), in 1969.

He lives in France. He has held several one-man exhibitions in London.

Examples of his sculpture are in Guildford Cathedral and King's College Chapel, Cambridge.

Coll : Manchester A.G.

Illustration in B.S.P.

SMITH, CHARLES LORAINE. 1751-1835

Squire of Enderby Hall, deputy Master of the Quorn, musician, poet, and M.P., this sportsman was an amateur artist of talent who recorded many famous hunting incidents in the Shires. He befriended Morland, having him to stay in an effort to break him from his London dissipation, and they worked together occasionally.

Loraine Smith, however, was more attracted to Henry Alken than to Morland, and Alken's influence is apparent in his hunting scenes.

He exhibited 6 works at R.A.

SMITH, H. C. op. 1820-1833

He painted portraits of dogs, game, and a few landscapes.

He exhibited 6 works at R.A., of which 2 were of dogs, 5 at B.I., 7 at S.S.

SMITH, JOHN HENRY. op. 1839-1893

One J. H. Smith engraved 'John Carlton and Fox-hounds' after R. B. Davis in 1839. It is not certain that he was the same man who started exhibiting in 1852 in London, showing landscape, genre, and pictures of animals.

He exhibited at the R.A., B.I., and S.S.

SMITH, J. L. op. 1832

He exhibited a horse-portrait at S.S. in that year.

SMITH, M. N. op. 1755

His portrait is extant of the Cullen Arabian, signed and dated 1755, in a classical setting with a Turkish groom, in the manner of Wootton. Spencer also painted this black horse.

Possibly he was one of Wootton's assistants: at present more is known about the stallion than about Smith.

SMITH, THOMAS. b. c.1720-1769

Smith 'of Derby' was one of the earlier landscape artists to paint his native countryside with distinction : in his case, the Peak district. Vivares engraved 40 of these works for Boydell. Others were engraved by Mason and by Elliott who was commissioned by Boydell to engrave six of Smith's pictures of horses.

He was the father of John Raphael Smith, the engraver.

SMITH, WILLIAM. op. 1813-1859

He started to exhibit at the R.A. and B.I. in 1813 and continued to do so well into the Victorian era. But his work remained typical of the first half of the 19th century, carefully observed and exact in detail. He did not confine himself to horse-portraiture – dogs, fish, and birds being included in his exhibits – nor to oils; he worked also in watercolour and etched some angling prints that were published in the Sporting Magazine. While he never reached the top class, he merits consideration among those below.

In 1840 he moved from London to Shropshire where it seems he lived for the rest of his life.

He exhibited 32 works at R.A., 15 at B.I., 7 at S.S., and 9 at O.W.C.S.

Coll : Reading.

SMYTHE, EDWARD ROBERT. 1810-1899

The elder son of an Ipswich Bank Manager, he worked there, moving to Bury St. Edmunds only in later life. He painted the East Anglian landscape and coastal scenery in a style that bore affinity to that of John Crome. His many pictures of horses, dogs, and other domestic animals are well painted and rise far above mere competence.

He exhibited 5 works at R.A., 4 at B.I., and 4 at S.S.

Coll : Exeter and Norwich A.G's.

SMYTHE, THOMAS. 1825-1907

Younger son of an Ipswich Bank Manager and brother of E. R., he too painted with merit the East Anglian landscape and coastal scenery, becoming particularly skilful at painting snow scenes.

Although horses and other animals frequently figure in his compositions, such as 'The Woodland Harriers' and 'Breaking-in Horses', he did not paint as many animal pictures as his brother.

He exhibited 3 works at R.A., and 17 at S.S.

Coll: Norwich A.G.

SNOW, JOHN WRAY. op. 1832-1840

This North Country artist painted sporting scenes, portraits of horses and of prize-winning cattle, and landscape in which cattle and sheep featured predominantly.

A mezzotint by J. Egan in 1833 after his 'Castle Howard Ox' exaggerated the animal's proportions in the typical contemporary manner.

C. Hunt made an aquatint in 1839 of his 'Harkaway, with Pedigree' and T. G. Lupton produced a mezzotint in 1840 of his 'Blagdon Meet'.

SPALDING, C. B. op. 1832-1868

Living at Reading and at Brighton, he made a successful career painting horses, equestrian groups, and battle scenes with more than average talent.

An early work was of a Foxhound bitch with her puppies, dated 1832: by 1840 he was exhibiting at the R.A. pictures of steeple-chasers belonging to John Elmore and in 1843 some horses of Sir E. Filmer.

His 'Meet of the Hambledon Hounds at Presaw' in 1844 with its individual portraits of men and horses displays considerable skill: it was engraved, with a key, by Day & Son. The following year his 'Thos. Scotland on Harricott' was lithographed by J. W. Giles and his 'Hampshire Hunt' of 1851 was lithographed by C. Moody. He was patronised by Queen Alexandria.

He painted many pictures of hunters and race-horses, including 'Satirist', the St. Leger winner of 1841, which was engraved by Charles Hunt.

He exhibited 5 works at R.A.

Col: Walker A.G.

SPENCER, THOMAS. op. 1700-1767

This old painter first made a reputation by painting portraits, miniatures, and on enamel. He should not be confused with Jarvis Spencer, a contemporary and successful portrait painter.

Finding horse portraiture most profitable, he worked with James Seymour and contributed to the set of 33 race-horses' portraits engraved by H. Roberts and published by J. Cheny between 1740 and 1746.

A folio published in 1752 called 'Horses and Pedigrees' contains engravings of his portraits of 'Silver Leg', 'Othello', 'Sporley', and 'Starling', with others by Seymour.

Another set engraved by R. Houston and published by Spencer and Clee in 1755/56 included his 'Crab', 'White Nose', the Cullen Arabian, and the Chestnut Arabian.

Thomas Butler published prints from his portraits between 1751 and 1755 which indicates that Spencer might have been one of Butler's unnamed assistants whose unsigned work has been attributed to their master.

SPERLING, J. W. op. 1845-1848

He painted portraits of horses and of their owners. He sent 3 works to the R.A. from a London address, the first being a portrait of a grey stallion belonging to the King of Wurtenburg.

SPILSBURY, EDGAR ASHE. op. 1800-1828

This talented amateur, who lived at Midhurst, painted horses, dogs, and wild animals in the style of Stubbs who died in 1806. There is no record that he ever studied under the Master but his influence was such that Spilsbury's work has sometimes been mistaken for that of Stubbs.

His exhibited pictures included 'The Tiger', 'Lion and Lioness', and 'Panthers and Leopards', while others entitled 'The Conquest of Horses', 'Horses Bathing from a Sea Shore', and 'Horses Greeting a Stranger' are subjects that Gilpin might well have chosen.

He exhibited 21 works at R.A. and 10 at B.I.

SPODE, JOHN. op. late 18th century – ?1835

The work of this painter is rare; usually it was of dogs in landscape settings in the manner of Reinagle.

Examples are 'Two Greyhounds and a Dead Hare' in a landscape, 'Setters in a Landscape' and a 'Gentleman on Horse-back with his Greyhounds', with Stonehenge in the background. A lithograph was made of his 'The Mare Nonpareil's Trotting Match'.

He had more talent than Sam Spode who may have been his son.

SPODE, SAMUEL. op. 1825-1858

This modest horse-painter sought a livelihood by painting clients' hunters in their loose-boxes and, more rarely, in the open. His moderate work is usually undated. Occasionally he painted race-horses, such as 'Berengaria', with Herbert Brown up, and 'Alice Hawthorn', depicted at the gallop.

He did not exhibit.

Two of his pictures were reproduced in the Sporting Magazine of 1825.

STARK, ARTHUR JAMES. 1831-1902

The son and pupil of the eminent landscapist James, he studied at the R.A. Schools, under E. Bristow (q.v.), and later, in 1874, with F. W. Keyl (q.v.).

Grant regretted that he did not absorb more of his father's influence but painted landscape in the slick, obvious Victorian manner. He became skilful in painting figures and animals which he often inserted in his father's compositions.

Among his R.A. exhibits, which were chiefly landscape, in 1863 he showed the portrait of a Hunter belonging to the Duke of Rutland.

He exhibited 35 works at R.A., 33 at B.I., and 51 at S.S.

Coll: V. & A., Exeter, Glasgow and Norwich A.G.

STEEL, JOHN SYDNEY. op. 1889-1900

This Londoner's exhibits were of red deer and elk. He painted moderate pictures of dogs. He sent 6 works to R.A., 5 to S.S., and 5 elsewhere.

STEELL, DAVID GEORGE, A.R.S.A. op. 1887-1890's

The son of Gourlay S. he likewise painted sporting genre, such as a 'Spaniel Guarding his Master's Game', but did not achieve the same degree of distinction as his father.

He exhibited 1 work at R.A.

STEELL, GOURLAY, R.S.A. 1819-1894

This eminent Scottish animalier was born in Edinburgh, the son of John Steell, an artist. His brother John became a sculptor of distinction and received a knighthood.

Steell was trained in art at the Galleries of the Board of Manufacturers. In 1855 he painted the portrait of 'Voltigeur', the Derby winner of 1850.

He did not start exhibiting at the R.A. until 1866, and submitted in 1871 an equestrian portrait of Col. Carrick Buchanan with Huntsman and Hounds. His last exhibit there was in 1874 of 4 of Queen Victoria's favourite dogs. He was made Animal Painter for Scotland to Her Majesty and Curator of the National Gallery of Scotland. He was the appointed painter of the Highland and Agricultural Society. He painted some historical and genre subjects.

He exhibited 10 works at R.A.

Coll: Glasgow A.G.

STEVENS, GEORGE. op. 1810-1865

This prolific artist painted animals, fruit, and game. The bulk of his output was shown at Suffolk Street. His R.A. exhibits included portraits of horses and in 1817 'A Deer Hunt'.

He exhibited 22 works at R.A. from 1810-1861, 75 at B.I., chiefly drawings, and 246 at S.A.

STILLWELL, J., Jnr. op. 1849-1855

He was a landscape and animal painter whose only exhibit at the R.A. was a portrait of a dog. His other exhibits included cattle. He lived at Tooting.

He exhibited 1 work at R.A., 4 at B.I., and 2 at S.S.

STOOP, JAN PETER. 1612-1685

A Dutch artist of this surname came to England from Portugal in 1662 in the suite of Catherine of

Braganza. He painted hunting and battle-scenes and views of sea-ports. He is best known for his etchings and engravings of horses and other animals; these have often been reprinted. He engraved, with Hollar, the plates for Ogilby's Aesop's Fables from his own and from Barlow's designs.

He died in England in 1685.

His elder brother Dirk Stoop painted hunters, horsemen, and farriers shops etc. in the manner of Wouvermans. Each used several first names and there are doubts if this does not cloak the identity of one man.

STOTT, J.   op. 1828-1830

Listed as a gem engraver, he exhibited 7 works at the R.A. His 'Tiger at Bay', 'Lion and Hottentot', and 'Heron' were all painted from sketches by Howitt. Another exhibit was 'Hunting Antelopes with a Panther'.

Coll: the Leeds A.G.

STRAFFORD, HENRY.   op. 1833-1873

Some of the work of this painter of pedigree stock was lithographed by J. W. Giles. This was done to advertise the merit of products of the cattle-breeders rather than that of the artist. An example is his picture of 4 sheep was at Gosfield Hall, Essex.

Hulmandel engraved his 'Castle Howard Oxen'. From 1842-1872 he was the proprietor of Coates' Herdbook, in which his lithograph of celebrated shorthorn cattle were published each year.

STRETTON, PHILIP EUSTACE.   op. 1884-1904

This Londoner painted chiefly dogs and sport. He started exhibiting at the R.A. in 1884. Among pictures submitted were 'After the Hunt', 'Portraits of Setters', and 'Puppyhood'.

He exhibited 18 works at R.A. and 3 at S.S.

STRUTT, ALFRED WILLIAM, R.B.A.   1856-1924

The son of William S., he was born in New Zealand. He was a pupil at the South Kensington School and started exhibiting at the R.A. in 1877. Working in oils and watercolours, he painted portraits, animals, and sport, exhibiting at S.S. and N.W.S. as well as R.A.

He went with Edward VII on a shooting trip to Scandinavia.

STRUTT, WILLIAM, R.B.A.   1826-1915

The son of William Thomas S., a miniature-painter, he was trained at the Beaux-Arts in Paris and became interested in painting animals.

In 1850 he went to Australia where his scenes of everyday life are interesting early records, reproduced in his 'Australian Journal' and 'Illustrated Australian Magazine'. He went to New Zealand in 1856 before returning to England in 1862.

He started exhibiting at the R.A. in 1865, showing portraits, genre, and religious subjects as well as animals. These last were painted with sympathy and ranged from portraits of horses, such as Lady Blunt's Arabian 'Sherila', to vast Victorian canvasses of the favourite subject of lions, such as 'A Pride of Lions before a Storm' and 'Lions attacking a Horseman'.

STUART, CHARLES, R.S.A.   op. 1888-1900

This Scot specialised in painting red deer in Highland forest landscape.

He should not be confused with the London landscape and marine artist or with the fruit, still life, and landscape artist, both of whom bore the same names.

He exhibited 5 works at R.A.

*STUBBS, GEORGE, A.R.A.   1724-1806

The son of a Liverpool tanner, he showed early interest in anatomy, receiving scant education in art. From 1744-1753 he painted portraits for a living in the North of England. During this period he lectured on human anatomy to students at York Hospital and drew and etched illustrations for a book on midwifery. He visited Italy in 1754.

For the next 4 years he was engaged on the tremendous work that resulted in his book 'The Anatomy of the Horse', doing dissections, writing, and illustrating it single-handed. Its publication in 1766 made his reputation as a 'horse-painter' although he was equally interested in other animals. His knowledge of anatomy and the rhythm of his composition, as exemplified in his pictures of Brood Mares and Foals, his superb draughtsmanship and sympathy with his subjects, combined to raise him far above other animal painters. He loved to paint exotic wild animals, while his conversation pieces of 18th century country gentry with their horses and dogs were never bettered.

It was, perhaps, his deep knowledge of anatomy that made him prefer to paint horses at rest: he must have realised from his studies that the usual 'rocking-chair' gallop was incorrect.

Horse-painters were considered unsuitable as founder-members of the R.A. so Stubbs turned to the F.S.A. and was elected Director in 1780, the year that he was belatedly made A.R.A. By then he was working for Wedgwood, using enamel colours on copper and on china plaques. Aged 78, and still at heart the anatomist, he started, but left unfinished, a comparative study of the Human Body with that of a Tiger and of the Common Fowl.

As English as the rural Thames, he is our greatest painter of animals.

Coll: V. & A., Tate, Fitzwilliam, the Walker, Birkenhead, Brighton, Leeds, and Manchester A.G's.
Illustration in B.S.P.

STUBBS, GEORGE TOWNLEY.   1756-1815

The natural son of the great George Stubbs, under whom he worked, he engraved some 36 prints after his father's pictures between 1770 and 1804. Amongst these were engravings of cattle which were published between 1788 and 1791.

His only exhibit at the R.A. in 1782 was a portrait of an old hunter. He is said to have made in watercolour good copies of some of his father's work.

Overshadowed by the genius of that great man, his career remains as obscure as his birth.

He exhibited 1 work at R.A., 3 at S.A.

STURGESS, JOHN.   op. 1869-1884

This artist worked for the 'Sporting and Dramatic News' as an illustrator of sporting events on the racecourse and in the hunting field. He also painted such episodes in oils. A set of four coloured aquatints of the 1872 Punchestown Conyingham Cup after him by E. G. Hester was published in 1874. He drew many of the illustrations in the Badminton Library volume on Hunting.

He exhibited 1 work at S.S.

SWAN, CUTHBERT EDMUND.   op. 1893-1900

The son of J. M. Swan, R.A., he became a member of the Feline School, painting, in oils and watercolours, wild animals of the cat tribe.

Among his R.A. exhibits were 'Duke', a study of a Lion, 'Jaguars at Play' and 'Puma and Cubs.'

He exhibited 4 works at R.A. from 1893.

SWAN, JOHN MACALLAN, R.A.   1847-1910

This eminent Victorian Painter and Sculptor was born of Scottish parents at Brentford. He studied at Worcester and Lambeth before proceeding to the R.A. schools and then worked in Paris under Gérôme and Fremiet. On his return to London he spent much time studying and drawing the animals in the Zoo and became a distinguished draughtsman and colourist.

He first exhibited at the R.A. in 1878; these early studies were of animals, especially lions, tigers, and other large cats. Later he produced idyllic compositions to include human figures in the nude. His 'Prodigal Son' was purchased for the Tate in 1888. He was elected full R.A. in 1905.

He turned more and more to modelling until he was devoting as much time to sculpture as to painting. He was a fastidious worker and his output was not great. His 'Walking Leopard' is at Manchester. He was commissioned to produce the 8 huge lions for the Rhodes monument at Capetown.

He gained early recognition on the Continent, receiving many awards, but his small output precluded him from greater popularity at home. On his death a fund was raised to purchase his many unfinished paintings and drawings of animals which were then distributed to many museums.

Coll: V. & A., Manchester A.G., and at Philadelphia.

TAIT, ARTHUR F.   1819-1905

A native of Liverpool, he studied at the Manchester Royal Institute. In 1850 he emigrated to the U.S.A. and became well-known as a painter of sporting scenes and of animals, producing work of fine quality.

He was made a full Academician of the National Academy of Design in 1858.

Many of his pictures were lithographed by Currier and Ives.

*TALBOYS, AGNES AUGUSTA. 1863-1941

A Bristolian, she became pre-eminent as a painter of cats, her work becoming well-known and reproduced throughout Europe and North America.

Her technique in painting the fur of these animals, especially the Persian breed, was outstanding, and this, with her ability to pose her subjects in playful incidents, appealed greatly to their numberless admirers.

Coll: Bristol A.G.

TAPPING, G. op. 1797-1799

This amateur artist exhibited 3 works at R.A. during these years, one of which was a Portrait of a Setter and another of a Nobleman's Groom.

TASKER, WILLIAM. 1808-1852

Born in London, he became a pupil of Robert Lorris of Chester where he spent the rest of his life.

He started his artistic career by painting views of that city but turned to painting portraits of horses and received commissions to paint many well-known race-horses. These were well-drawn and were often set with a crowded race-course as background, thereby adding considerably to the interest of his compositions. 'Milipede' with Benby up, at Chester Race-course, is a good example of his work.

His picture of 1837 of a shooting pony with dogs and dead game compares favourably with later Victorian variations of this theme.

TAYLER, JOHN FREDERICK, P.R.W.S. 1802-1889

Son of a Hertfordshire country gentleman, he studied at Sass's Academy and the R.A. schools before going to Horace Vernet's studio in Paris. He shared a studio with Bonnington and after further study in Rome, returned to England on Bonnington's death in 1823. Though essentially a watercolourist, he was equally successful in oils.

He became well-known for his Scottish sporting scenes, painted with grace and charm and seldom spoilt by the sentimentality which blighted the work of his contemporary Landseer. He also produced many pastoral and historical scenes.

He was President of the Old Water Colour Society from 1858-1871.

He exhibited 5 works at R.A., 5 at B.I., and 360 at the O.W.C.S.

Coll: V. & A., Newcastle and Manchester A.G.'s.

TAYLOR, STEPHEN. op. 1817-1837

He worked in Winchester, Oxford, and London. His pictures are seldom seen despite his list of exhibits which included many of game-birds, some of large size, and of wild animals.

He also painted sporting pictures of dogs and portraits of horses: that of the hunter 'Curricle' being an example.

He should not be confused with another S. Taylor who exhibited portraits from 1838-1849.

He exhibited 39 works at R.A., 28 at B.I., 40 at S.S.

*THOMPSON, RALPH. living artist

Born in Yorkshire, he studied at the Leeds College of Art and at the Royal College of Art, London.

As a freelance illustrator he specialises in pictures of Wild Life, albeit his subjects were studied in British Zoos.

He described this side of his work in 'A Brush with Animals', published in 1963.

In 1954 he began a long associaton with Gerald Durrell whose 'Bafut Beagles' he illustrated that year.

He has appeared on television and has held his own exhibition in London at the Tryon Gallery.

Coll: Belfast A.G.

THOMSON, JOHN MURRAY, R.S.W. 1885 - op. 1934

Animal painter. Former President S.S.A. Studied art in Scotland and Paris.

Exhibited at R.A. and R.S.A.

*THORBURN, ARCHIBALD. 1860-1935

Born in Dumfries, the son of the miniaturist, Robert Thorburn, A.R.A., he went to London where he became a popular illustrator and painter of birds. He was friends with other naturalist-artists like George Lodge and Joseph Wolf under whose influence he came.

For Lord Lilford he illustrated 'Game Birds and Waterfowl', 'British Birds' and 'British Mammals'.

Although watercolour was his usual medium and birds his usual subjects, occasionally he painted pictures of dogs and deer.

He exhibited 16 works at R.A., and 1 at S.S.

Coll: Belfast, Blackburn, Edinburgh, and Preston A.G's.

Illustration in B.S.P.

TILLEMANS, PETER. 1684-1734

Born in Antwerp, the son of a diamond cutter, he was brought to England with Casteels in 1708 by a picture-dealer called Turner who employed him in copying Old Masters. From this occupation he passed to painting topographical views, often in watercolour, of the country seats of the nobility and gentry by whom he was well patronised. In these pictures he took to inserting horses, deer, and hounds. In 1719 he was employed by John Bridges to make 500 drawings in Indian ink for his 'History and Antiquities of Northamptonshire'.

In 1722 he painted a large panoramic picture of Geo. I and his Court on Newmarket Heath in which both the humans and horses are portraits. He did many more such scenes and many portraits of race-horses, some of which are indistinguishable from those of Wootton. If Barlow was the Father of Sporting Art in England, Tillemans and Wootton must be counted as its god-parents.

Illustrated in B.S.P.

*TIMYM, WILLIAM. 1912 - living artist

Born in Vienna, he studied drawing and sculpture at the Academy of Arts. Several of his exhibitions were held there and at Cologne. In 1938 he came to England where he has made his name with his portrait sculpture, his studies of wild animals, and his programme on television.

In 1938 his bronze of Sir Malcolm Sargent was exhibited at the Royal Festival Hall.

His animal drawings and sculpture have been shown at the Moorland Gallery since 1970.

TINNE, DOROTHEA. b. 1899

Studied St. John's Wood Schools and in Amsterdam. Animal painter, signs work 'E. D. Tinne'.

TOLLEY (TOLLY), EDWARD. op. 1848-1867

This dedicated painter of horses showed pictures entitled 'A Favourite Hunter', 'Study of Horses', and 'Favourite Hunters at Cover-side', only deviating once to include a Lion amongst his œuvre.

He exhibited 9 works at R.A., 3 at B.I., and 1 at S.S.

TOMSON, J. CLIFTON (or THOMSON) op. 1775-1831

This Nottingham sporting painter produced many portraits of hunters and race-horses for such patrons as Lord Fitzwilliam. Those of the more celebrated winners of the turf were frequently reproduced in the Old Sporting Magazine, the first appearing in Vol. 18 of 1801. He worked mostly in the Midlands and Yorkshire where he painted portraits of the stallions 'Selim' and 'Evander' in 1811. His portrait of the race-horse 'Orville', dated 1812, was engraved by J. Scott.

His work can be regarded as competently professional rather than of high artistic merit. He never exhibited in London.

Coll: Walker and Nottingham A.G's.

TOWNE, CHARLES. 1763-1840 'of Liverpool'

Two unrelated artists of this name painted the same subjects during the same period. The elder is known as Towne of Liverpool.

Born in Wigan, as a youth he worked for a short spell with John Rathbone, the landscapist, in Leeds, before going to Manchester where necessity forced him to work as a coach-painter and japanner. At 17 he set up on his own, painting horses. A spell of 3 or 4 years in London and Essex broadened his experience in art and life and added considerably to his reputation as a painter of horses and cattle. His love of the Dutch masters is reflected in the landscape settings of these pictures, displaying more talent than the subjects themselves merited. He returned from the South to settle in Liverpool and added the 'e' to his name.

Pot-Boilers apart, at his best in this latest period, he was considered by Grant the most artistic of our animal painters, able to please both connoisseur and cattle-owner with the same picture.

He exhibited 7 works at R.A., 30 at Liverpool, 1 at B.I.

66

Coll: the Walker and Birkenhead A.G's.
Illustration in B.S.P.

TOWNSHEND, ARTHUR LOUIS.   op. 1880-1887
This Victorian horse-painter worked at Newmarket, London, and Paris, his subjects being race-horses and blood-stock. In 1885 he sent to the R.A. 'Janette and her Foal' and 'The Gem of the Paddocks'. His portrait of 'Bird of Freedom', winner of the Ascot Queen's Vase of 1886 and of the Gold Cup of 1887, was well-painted.
He sent 5 works to the R.A.

TRERY, HENRY C.   op. 1849-1854
He painted dogs, sheep, cattle, and deer. His R.A. exhibit of 1853 was 'Study of a Dog's Head', while that of 1854 was 'Red Deer'.
He sent 5 works to the R.A. and 1 to B.I.

TULLOCH, MAURICE, Colonel.   living artist
In addition to painting portraits of horses, this Indian Cavalry officer has drawn and painted many sporting incidents observed in the course of his service. As an illustrator, he can represent, in an individual style, horses in movement with great economy of line.

TUNNICLIFFE, CHARLES FREDERICK, R.A.   1901 - living artist
Born near Macclesfield, he became a prominent etcher and painter in oils and watercolours of animals, birds, and fish, after winning the Royal Exhibition Scholarship to the Royal College of Arts in 1921. He started exhibiting at the R.A. in 1928 and was made full R.A. in 1954. He did much engraving and book illustrating.
He has held his own exhibitions in London since 1963 and his publications include 'My Country Book' in 1942 and 'Bird Portraiture' in 1945.
He has exhibited at R.A. from 1928.
Coll: the Manchester and Belfast A.G's.

TURNER, F. C., R.B.A.   1795-1846
The 'clubable' friend of many of his contemporaries, he was widely known as an illustrator in such periodicals as the Old Sporting Magazine, in which 78 of his works were published. He painted many portraits of race-horses, hunters, and hounds as well as sporting scenes, some on large canvasses. He exhibited at the R.A. from 1817. One of his most attractive portraits was of Master Beecher on the celebrated pony, 'Lady-bird', exhibited in 1836. He painted the portraits of 'Little Wonder' and 'Coronation', winners of the Derby in 1840 and 1841.
Turner's wooden leg proved no handicap to his eye or brush.
He exhibited 11 works at R.A., 23 at B.I., 36 at S.S.
Coll: the Manchester and Walker A.G's.
Illustration in B.S.P.

TURNER, G. A.   op. 1838-1841
One of the sons of F. C. Turner, he was hailed as a 'talented young artist and a chip off the old block', on the publication in the Sporting Magazine of 1838 of a plate from his 'Bellman', a Highland Deerhound. He was unable to live up to this puff and only 3 other plates from him appeared in that periodical.
He made some prints after his father: the St. Leger 1839, the Wolverhampton Stakes, and the race-horse 'Refraction' are recorded.
His work is characterised by a high finish.
He exhibited 3 works at R.A., 1 at B.I., and 2 at S.S.

TURNER, W. H. M.   op. 1860-1887
He painted portraits of horses on panel or small canvasses. A 'Greyhounds Coursing a Hare' is recorded.
He lived at Bath.
He exhibited one picture of cattle at S.S. in 1860.

*UNDERWOOD, T. op. *c.* 1844-1849

A roan and white Shorthorn Bull in a landscape was painted by him in 1844 as well as 'A Prize Angus Bull' and 'A Roan Shorthorn Bull'. He ran a lithographic establishment in Birmingham. One of his plates was of Prize Cattle at the Birmingham & Midland Counties Exhibition of 1849.

VAN DIEPENBECK, ABRAHAM. 1596-1675

In 1629 this Flemish pupil of Rubens was commissioned by the Duke of Newcastle to paint a series of a dozen portraits of his horses at Welbeck. He was one of the earliest foreigners to influence our native artists. Wootton and Stubbs both painted at Welbeck and must have been familiar with at least one of these portraits which still remains in the Collection of the Duke of Portland.

In 1657 Newcastle published his 'New Method to Dress Horses' with illustrations from Van Diepenbeck. He died at Antwerp in 1675.

VEAL, GEORGE. op. 1893

A portrait of 'Hardcash', with jockey up, and his trainer, was painted by him in this year.

VERNER, FREDERICK ARTHUR. op. 1881-1900

This Canadian, who came from Ottawa, exhibited pictures of animals in London from 1881-1900.

VILLIERS, FRANCOIS HUET. 1772-1813

This French refugee was a miniaturist of note who exhibited 130 works in London from 1803-1813. Among these were pictures in watercolour of animals. That his father had been an animal painter in Paris accounts for this diversion.

VINE, JOHN. op. *c.*1842-1861

Only bare mention need be made of this Colchester painter. His portrait of a dark bay horse in a loose box must be classified as provincial, painted too late to be called primitive.

'A Large White Pig' and 'Lord Weston's Devon Ox' are also recorded.

He sent a 'Farmyard' to the S.S. in 1844.

VINNE, JAN VAN DER. 1663-1721

This pupil of Jan Wyck came to England in 1686 from Harlem where he returned to die. He painted hunting and racing scenes, as well as a few landscapes, but did not display the talents of his master.

Illustration in B.S.P.

WAIN, LOUIS WILLIAM. 1860-1939

A Londoner, at 19 he turned from the study of music to that of drawing at the West London School of Art where he became an assistant master. From there he joined the staff of the 'Illustrated Sporting and Dramatic News' and later the 'Illustrated London News'. He worked in New York from 1907 to 1910.

He became extremely popular as a painter of cats and was elected President of the National Cat Club.

An exhibition of his numerous drawings and illustrations was held at the Victoria & Albert Museum in 1972. He died insane. His biography was published byRodney Dale in 1968.

He exhibited a picture at S.S. in 1889.

WAINEWRIGHT, THOMAS GRIFFITH. op. 1821-1825

The pictures sent by him from a London address are recorded as being of cattle.

He may have been the father of John Wainewright, who painted flowers, and Thomas Francis Wainewright who painted landscape.

He exhibited 6 works at R.A. and 1 at B.I.

WALKER, J. F. op. 1867-1889

The work of this provincial artist, who lived in Hull, is rare. He painted equestrian groups, an example being a Meet of the Hounds of Sir Thomas Constable, for whom he painted several pictures at Burton Constable. A Prize Bull in a landscape is recorded.

WALLACE, DONALD C. living artist

This artist has spent several years in Central Africa and portrays the wild life of those regions, especially lions and elephants.

WALLACE, HAROLD FRANK. 1881-1962

Educated at Eton and Christchurch, he was called to the Bar in 1908. He lived in Staffordshire and Inverness and painted many pictures of red deer and of angling. An expert stalker, he worked in watercolour and illustrated numerous articles in black and white on his favourite subject, which, set in well-painted Highland scenery, gave them great authenticity.

He was Deer Controller for Scotland during World War II.

WALLS, WILLIAM, R.S.A., R.W.S. 1860-1942

After leaving Edinburgh Academy, this Scot was a student at the R.A. Schools and in Antwerp. A comparatively late arrival to the Feline School, he frequented the London and Antwerp Zoos to make excellent studies of the wild animals therein. He worked in oils and watercolours.

Mostly he exhibited at R.W.S. (elected 1906) and at the R.S.A., of which he became a full member in 1914, sending only 4 works to the R.A. These included the 'Fox's Lair', 'Bolting the Otter', and 'Jaguar Stalking'.

His 'Puma Startled' was shown at the R.S.A. Centenary Exhibition of 1926.

Coll: the V. & A.; Edinburgh.

WALTER, HENRY. 1786-1849

This Londoner was a teacher of painting and drawing. He compiled lithographed drawing books for students that contained studies of domestic animals done with great skill.

He set himself a high standard, ruthlessly destroying those of his efforts that did not attain it.

He painted genre and landscape as well as animals; in depicting the latter he showed sympathy and great knowledge.

He was a friend of John Linnell, Snr., and of William Blake.

He exhibited at R.A. (6), B.I. (6), S.S. (2), N.W.C.S. (3).

He showed at R.A. in 1822 'An Old Hunter' and in 1833 'Study of a Bull'.

*WARD, JAMES, R.A. 1769-1859

The pupil of his brother William, and apprenticed to John Raphael Smith, the engraver, he soon distinguished himself in their field. By 1787 he had turned to painting domestic subjects in the manner of his brother-in-law Morland, but from 1797 his own powerful wiry style, with its brilliant colouring and virile execution, began to emerge. In 1794 he was appointed Painter and Mezzotint Engraver to the Prince of Wales. Success as an animal painter led to his being commissioned by the Agricultural Society to paint 200 portraits of the native breeds of cattle, pigs, and sheep. Due to the failure of Boydell, the publisher, this project was never completed but it brought Ward into contact with the foremost breeders of the day and he was showered with commissions.

Ambitious to be more than a cattle-painter, a sight of Rubens 'Chateau de Stein' inspired him to paint 'Fighting Bulls at St. Donat's Castle' and later, the huge 'Gordale Scar'. but his religious and allegorical subjects were failures. He was made A.R.A. in 1807, the year that he began painting thoroughbreds, and was profitably occupied with commissions for these for several years. He was advanced to full R.A. in 1811. Tough and hard-working, he was prolific in many fields and must be counted in the first rank of our animal painters. Regretfully, he lived to be 90, into the age of Landseer, and suffered from declining powers and health for the last 25 years of his life.

He exhibited 298 works at R.A., 91 at B.I., 2 at S.A., 9 at S.S.

Coll: Nat. Gallery, V. & A., the Tate, the Fitzwilliam, Bristol, Cardiff, Leeds, Southampton, Whitworth, York, Plymouth, Nottingham A.G's, and in the Mellon Collection.

Illustration in B.S.P.

WARD, MARTIN THEODORE. 1799-1874

Son of William Ward, the engraver, he was a pupil of his famous uncle James with whom he lived for a time, but the genius did not rub off on him and his work remains honest but undistinguished.

His London exhibits from 1819 to 1858 were portraits of horses and dogs in landscape.

He died in straitened circumstances at York.

He exhibited 16 works at R.A., and 18 at B.I.

Coll: the Preston A.G.

*WARDLE, ARTHUR, R.I.   1864-1949

Working in oils, watercolour, and pastel, he painted domestic and wild animals and many sporting scenes. He excelled with his studies in pastel of wild animals of the feline tribe.

He had an exhibition at Vicars in 1935.

He exhibited 21 works at R.A. from 1880-1935, 29 at S.S., 20 at N.W.C.S.

Coll: The Tate and the Leeds A.G.

WATSON, WILLIAM, Jnr.   op. from 1866-d.1923

This Liverpool painter of landscape and animals, son of a miniaturist of the same name, was a pupil of Landseer and Rosa Bonheur.

In 1872 he submitted 'Scotch Cattle' to the R.A. He sent 1 other work to S.S.

Coll: the Birkenhead, Liverpool, Manchester, Sheffield, and Sunderland A.G's.

WEAVER, JOHN PYEFINCH.   op. 1801-1809

The son of Thomas Weaver, he sent 4 exhibits to the R.A., the first in 1801, a landscape with cattle. In 1808 he submitted portraits of Lord Anson's Long-horned Bull and Lady Anson's favourite mare. The following year a portrait of a celebrated Carthorse, 'Bobtail', was shown.

*WEAVER, THOMAS.   1774-1843

Born at Worthen, Salop, he did not receive any formal education in art. He developed a wide range of subjects, painting portraits, sporting scenes, and occasional landscape, but is best known for his portraits of horses and pedigree cattle. Shaw Sparrow considered that in this branch he was greatly influenced by Stubbs. The purpose of many of these commissions was to publicise the products of the pioneer breeders, so their grotesque appearance must not be taken to indicate the artist's lack of anatomical knowledge. Much of his work in this field was engraved by William Ward and Richard Woodman.

Among his early patrons was the famous animal-breeder, Thomas Coke of Holkham – his masterpiece is of this patron with his shepherd and examples of his improved flock of sheep.

He exhibited in London from 1801 to 1814 and in 1822 at Liverpool where he died.

He exhibited 4 works at R.A.

Coll: Reading.

WEBB, BYRON.   op. 1846-1866

A son of Archibald Webb, Snr., the marine painter, with whom he lived in Chelsea, he became a high-class painter of animals, equestrian groups, and hunting scenes. His portraits display his command of anatomy while the settings of these and of his pictures of deer are equally well-painted, as shown in his 'Edmund Tattersall on Black Bess' and the Queen's 'Abdallah' of 1854.

He exhibited 11 works at R.A., 16 at B.I., 8 at S.S.

WEBB, E. W.   ?1805-1854

Related to Archibald and Byron Webb, he painted animals and sporting scenes. He did much of his work at Leamington where he gained commissions painting portraits of horses in a sound but uninspiring manner.

He exhibited 1 at R.A., 1 at B.I.

Coll: Walker A.G.

WEBB, WILLIAM.   op. 1819-1855

This not unimportant animal painter lived at Tamworth, Staffs., and was originally a clock-maker. He is best known for his portraits of race-horses and hunters, though he painted wild animals, equestrian portraits, sporting, and occasional historical subjects. His talents lifted him above the majority of his fellows, a fine example of his virile style being his picture of the race-horse 'Euphrates' in the Mellon Collection; while of his equestrian portraits that of the eccentric John Mytton is a good example.

Until the end of his career he was well-patronised, painting portraits of hunters at Melton Mowbray.

He exhibited 7 works at R.A., 1 at B.I.

Coll: Mellon Collection and Walker A.G.

Illustration in B.S.P.

WEEKES, HENRY.   op. 1849-1888

One of the 5 artistic children of Henry, W., R.A., the sculptor, he painted animals, rural genre, and views of Hampstead Heath. He started exhibiting at R.A. in 1851; titles submitted included 'A Dairy Stable' and 'Fancy Rabbits'.

He exhibited 26 works at R.A., 17 at B.I., 18 at S.S.

Coll: Leeds A.G.

*WEEKES, WILLIAM. op. 1864-1904

The humorous member of the family of Henry W., R.A., the sculptor, he started exhibiting at the R.A. in 1865 and later at B.I. and S.S. His subjects were domestic and farmyard animals in comical situations of the Couldery (*q.v.*) School. But his passion was for painting donkeys in this vein, of which 'The Connoisseurs' — 5 donkeys standing round a picture on a easel — is a fair example.

He exhibited 49 works at R.A., 11 at B.I., 10 at S.S.

WEIR, HARRISON WILLIAM. 1824-1906

Born at Lewes, he studied colour-printing under George Baxter but left this to become an artist. He gained great popularity as a sympathetic illustrator and draughtsman of animals and birds, working for the 'Illustrated London News', the Graphic', and other periodicals. He wrote and illustrated many books, including 'Poultry and All About Them'. A keen naturalist, he was a friend of Darwin and had great scientific knowledge of the animals and birds that he loved.

His first wife was the eldest daughter of J. F. Herring.

He exhibited 6 works at R.A., 3 at B.I., 4 at S.S.

A drawing and 3 of his sketch-books are in the V. & A.

WELLES, E. F. op. 1826-1856

He lived in Worcestershire, Hereford, and London, painting animals and landscape. He started exhibiting at the R.A. in 1826, sending a portrait of the race-horse 'Manfred'. Other titles submitted were 'Study of a Horse's Head' and a 'Landscape with Cattle'.

In about 1835 he produced 25 etched plates of cattle.

WHAITE, T. op. 1834-1835

Two portraits of race-horses painted by him are recorded: 'Touchstone', ridden by Calloway, who won the St. Leger in 1834, and 'Queen of Trumps', with Lye up, winner of the Oaks and St. Leger in 1835.

WHEELER, ALFRED. op. 1862-1898

A son of J. A. Wheeler of Bath, he had more talent than his brother James and received commissions to paint some famous race-horses as well as the usual hunters. He painted such classic winners as 'Ladas' and 'Persimmon' and the matches between 'The Bard' and 'Rosicrucius' and 'The Bard' and 'Ormonde'.

WHEELER, JAMES ?F. (Junior) op. 1860-1880's

A son of J. A. Wheeler, Snr., of Bath, he also painted sport and portraits of horses, usually hunters, in a manner similar but inferior to his father's. His father signed his work J. Wheeler or used the monogram J.W. which accounts for the use of 'senior' and 'junior' to distinguish them.

WHEELER, JOHN ARNOLD. (Senior) 1821-1904 'Of Bath'

This sound provincial animal painter, born near Andoversford, was self-taught. He started his career in the Army, becoming a bandsman in the Queen's Bays, where he developed his natural talent and learnt to paint horses with accuracy. When he left the Army in 1857, he settled in Bath where he made a name painting hunting and racing scenes as well as portraits of horses and dogs.

His best known works were of 'The Beaufort Hunt' and 'The Meet of the Coaching Club, London' in which humans, horses, and hounds were all portraits. He was well patronised by the aristocracy and by sportsmen. He went to London in 1877 and died in Hanwell.

Coll: Victoria A.G., Bath.

Illustration in B.S.P.

WHESSEL, JOHN. 1760-?1823

He became better-known as an engraver on copper — making plates after Gainsborough, Stothard, Singleton and Serres — than a painter. As such he had ability: besides landscapes and subject pictures, he painted some portraits of horses. He engraved Boultbee's 'Durham Ox' and other cattle portraits. He worked at Oxford.

He exhibited 14 works at the R.A., including, in 1805, 'Eagle' beating 'Eleanor' at Newmarket, in 1807, Lord Egremont's 'Bobtail' and the Duke of Grafton's 'Parasol', and in 1808, Lord Sackville's 'Dick Anden' and Lord Grosvenor's 'Violante'. All were engraved by J. Deeley in 1814.
His last exhibit was in 1823 of a 'General View of Oxford'.

WHITFORD, R.   op. 1854-1886
This Victorian animal-painter was employed in producing the portraits of prize animals. Heifers, bulls, cart-horses, and the occasional hunter, often painted in landscape settings, were his subjects.
He painted two Shire Horses who won first prize at the Warwick R.A.S. in 1859.
Coll: Reading.

WHITING, FREDERIC, R.S.W., R.I.   b. 1874 - op. 1945
After studying at St. John's Wood, the R.A. schools, and at Julian's in Paris, he worked as an illustrator for the 'Graphic' during the Russo-Japanese War of 1904-5.
Later he became well-known for his pictures of horses before making his name as a portrait and figure painter. He showed regularly at the R.A. and at the Salon. One of his most successful works was of the Princesses riding at Windsor in 1945.
Examples of his work are in the Brighton, Glasgow, Liverpool, and Wolverhampton A.G's.

WHITMARSH, ELIZA.   (Mrs. T. H.)   op. 1840-1851
This lady was an amateur genre artist who included in her œuvre portraits of horses and dogs.
She sent 8 works to R.A., and one each to B.I. and S.S.

WHYMPER, CHARLES, R.I.   1853-1941
This prolific illustrator depicted in the Big Game Shooting volume of the Badminton Library much of the varied fauna of Africa, either at peace or reacting dramatically to our blood-thirsty forebears.
He was a pupil of Joseph Wolf.
He exhibited 5 works at R.A., 1 at S.S., 2 at N.W.C.S.

WIDDAS, JOHN.   1802-1858
A native of Hull, he painted horses and dogs in well-executed settings. His pure landscape was more topographical than artistic.
He was the father of R. D. Widdas.

WIDDAS, RICHARD DODD.   1826-1885
A resident of Hull, he painted portraits of horses and dogs as well as sporting and shipping scenes. He was a son of John W.
Coll: The Hull Museum.

WIDGERY, WILLIAM.   1822-1893
This Exeter stone-mason taught himself to be a painter of animals and landscape. He did sufficiently well reproducing Landseer's 'Monarch of the Glen' to take up art professionally.
His landscapes of Devon and Cornwall became popular locally. His picture of the Poltimore Hunt was engraved by J. Harris.
He sent only 1 work to S.S.

WIGHTMAN, THOMAS.   1811-1888
Although mostly he painted racing subjects, occasionally he painted portraits of horses; one of these was 'Elis', St. Leger winner of 1836, also painted by Cooper and Herring.
He died in New York.

WILLIAMS, WILLIAM.   op. 1763-1800
This early painter of rustic out-door scenes in the genre of Morland and Biggs was popular in his day, exhibiting 30 works at the R.A. and 18 at S.A. and F.S., sent from Shrewsbury, Manchester, Norwich and London. These included scenes from the poets and portraits, as well as landscape. He painted the occasional hunting scene and portraits of horses. In the latter he was more successful in depicting the jockeys and the background than the actual subjects: these are somewhat wooden.

WILLIS, Henry Brittan, R.W.S.   1810-1884

The son of a Bristol drawing master, he became a popular painter of landscape with cattle. He has been compared favourably with that other successful Victorian pastoralist, Sydney Cooper.

He worked in oils and watercolour, being made a full member of the O.W.S. in 1863. Queen Victoria bought his 'Highland Cattle' of 1866.

He exhibited 27 works at R.A., 18 at B.I., 14 at S.S., and 366 at O.W.S.

Coll: V. & A., Bristol, Birmingham, Leicester, York A.G's.

WILLOUGHBY, W. WILLOUGHBY.   op. 1857-1888

It seems that this painter was an amateur. He worked at Boston. A chestnut hunter in a landscape and a Sherling Ram bred by Mr. Wilson of Stickford are recorded.

He did not exhibit in London.

WILSON, ALEXANDER.   op. 1803-1846

He was an animal painter long resident in Manchester.

WILSON, G. A.   op. 1806-1808

In 1808 he painted the race-horse 'Roseden' in a landscape, at Newcastle. This horse had won the Carlisle Steeplechase in 1806.

WILSON, THOMAS FAIRBAIRN.   op. *c.*1808-1846

This painter of portraits, landscape, and animals was distinguished from others by the sobriquet 'Wilson of Hull'.

His early portrait of 'Little Tan', a grey cob of 18 years, was painted well enough.

Coll: Reading.

WINGFIELD, J.   op. 1791-1798

This unimportant 18th century artist painted animals, birds, fish, and flowers, often in landscape settings. His 'Death of a Hare' appeared in 1797.

He exhibited 8 works at R.A.

WOLF, JOSEPH, R.I.   1820-1899

Born near Coblenz, from childhood he was fascinated in studying and drawing birds. After apprenticeship in Coblenz, he worked as a lithographer at Darmstadt before going to Antwerp and in 1848 to London where he remained for life.

Here he was employed at the B.M. and illustrated many books on natural history, such as Gould's 'Birds of Great Britain' and 'Birds of Asia', and the volume on Big Game Shooting of the Badminton Library. But though a naturalist of great distinction, he was also an artist whose work in oils is outstanding for its fine colour and tone. In his compositions of wild animals in their natural surroundings his creation of atmosphere has seldom been bettered. His charcoal studies of birds were distinguished by a lightness of touch that in no way detracted from the accuracy of detail.

His 'Life' was published by A. H. Palmer in 1895.

He exhibited 14 works at R.A., 7 at B.I., 20 at N.W.C.S.

Coll: B.M., Belfast A.G.

WOLSTENHOLME, DEAN.   1757-1837

Misfortune brought renown to this Yorkshire country gentleman and sportsman when, after losing three expensive law-suits in middle age, he turned his amateur talent for drawing to professional account. Self-taught but determined, he fulfilled Reynold's earlier remark that he would be a painter.

In 1803 his first picture, 'Coursing', was accepted by the R.A.

He became known for his interior scenes with animals and for his painting of brewery-yards with their dray-horses – subjects also painted by his son of the same name. Portraits of race-horses, hunt groups, and hunting scenes, and cattle portraits of inferior merit, flowed from his brush. Their landscape settings were painted with vigour, though often dark and gloomy in contrast to Dean junior, whose backgrounds are bright and sunny. Their careers overlapped by 8 years and their style at this time was similar. A sportsman, Dean senior, was in full sympathy with his subjects. His work reflects the straightness of his character.

He exhibited 26 works at R.A., the last in 1824.
Illustration in B.S.P.
Coll: The Walker A.G.

WOLSTENHOLME, C. DEAN. 1798-1883
Unlike his father of the same name, he was trained for his profession and surpassed him in skill. In his early phase he too painted brewery-yards and their dray-horses in a more exact style than his father did. Only occasionally did he include the 'C' in his signature, which has led to confusion.
His reputation rests secure as a sporting artist. He also painted many portraits of dogs and horses and engraved both his own and his father's work.
Exhibited 13 at R.A., 10 at B.I., 13 at S.S.
Coll: Walker A.G.

*WOODHOUSE, WILLIAM. 1857-1939
Born near Morecambe, he studied at the Lancaster School of Art. In 1899 he toured the Near East, visiting Greece and Turkey.
He seldom exhibited outside Lancashire, contributing works regularly, from 1927 till his death, to the Lancashire Art Exhibition. A memorial exhibition in 1939 at Preston showed 89 of his works, mostly of animals, of which he was a competent painter.
He exhibited 2 pictures at R.A. in 1889 and 1896.

WOODROUFFE, R. op. 1835-1854
He painted game-birds and animals, his favourite subjects being deer in the Highlands.
He exhibited 4 works at R.A. and 4 at B.I.

WOODWARD, THOMAS. 1801-1852
The son of a Pershore solicitor, his gifts were recognised by Benjamin West and he was sent as a pupil to Abraham Cooper. His close study of animals resulted in his portraits of dogs and horses being well modelled and true to life with their landscape settings finely done. He became an intimate friend of Landseer who once wished he 'could paint a horse like Woodward' and who obtained Royal patronage for him. His lively pictures of children with ponies are painted with great sympathy and gusto.
He became best known for his historical battle-scenes in which horses were prominent, such at 'The Battle of Worcester' and 'The Struggle for the Standard'. He first exhibited at the R.A. in 1821. 'Mazeppa' was exhibited in 1828.
Had he not died in early middle age, he would have joined the front rank of his profession.
He showed 85 works at the R.A., 60 at B.I., 15 at S.S.

WOOLCOTT, D. op. 1828-1840
Recorded as a painter of animals, he exhibited at the R.A. in 1828 a 'Horse and Groom'.

WOOLLETT, HENRY A. op. 1851-1873
This London landscape painter frequently included well-painted horses in his rural compositions.
A 'Huntsman and Hounds' is recorded.
He exhibited at S.S. and other galleries.

WOOTTON, FRANK. 1914 - living artist
This Hampshire-born artist studied at the Eastbourne College of Art where he gained a travelling scholarship. He paints animals, sport, and landscape. During the War he was an Official War Artist to the R.A.F. His work includes studies of horses, equestrian groups, and racing scenes. He has travelled widely abroad executing commissions
He has exhibited at the R.A. and other galleries and has had exhibitions in London.

WOOTTON, JOHN. 1677?-1765
Pupil, and later assistant, to Jan Wyck, the painter of battle and hunting-scenes, he worked in 1694 with the landscape artist Siberechts. After Wyck's death in 1702 Wootton set up at Newmarket where by 1714 he had made a great reputation with the nobility as a painter of horse portraits and racing scenes on the Heath. In 1720 the Duke of Beaufort enabled him to travel to Rome to study – an important event in his career.

Vertue records that after his return, in the period 1721-25, he was painting classical landscape in the manner of Claude and Gaspar Poussin. Later in life he did so more frequently.

Wootton's genius and the broad education in art that he received was to make him the founder of the traditional English school of sporting art. He was no mere horse-painter: contemporay opinion held that the ex-amateur James Seymour was better than he at conveying a horse's individuality. His style in portraying horses, often demanded on large canvasses in classical settings, did not alter much after 1714.

An equally important, though indirect, result of his achievement was its effect on landscape painting in England. He greatly influenced his pupil, George Lambert, called the 'Father of the English Landscape', who in turn influenced the young Richard Wilson.

Coll: The Fitzwilliam, Tate, and York A.G.

Illustration in B.S.P.

WRIGHT, GEORGE. 1856-1942

A brother of Gilbert, the sporting illustrator, he worked in Leeds, Oxford, and Rugby, painting hunting, coaching, and other sporting scenes, and, more rarely, portraits of horses.

He was a master at portraying the actual paces of a horse as disclosed by photography, whether walking or trotting. This gives his work the realism that is lacking in that of many of his contemporaries.

He exhibited frequently at R.A.

Coll: Walker A.G.

Illustration in B.S.P.

WRIGHT, T. op. 1750's

Little is known of this competent early artist who produced a fine picture in the style of Wootton, of the Gold Cup at Newmarket, 1751. It is entitled 'Le Course de Newmarket. T. Wright, Londres'.

Other pictures that he painted were a portrait of 'Son of Childers', held by a Groom with Jockey approaching on a Grey, now believed to be in the U.S.A., and of 'Brisk' whose picture was also painted by Thos. Butler or his assistants.

WYCK, JAN. 1652-1702

Born in Haarlem he accompanied his father Thomas to England in the reign of Charles II, married, and remained here for life. He became a distinguished painter of battle and sporting scenes, often large in size. His smaller pictures were of better quality and sometimes masterly. He has been called the Dutch father of the first English landscape tradition. He illustrated a book on Hunting and Hawking.

Though he could paint a horse with accuracy and spirit, his inclusion in this volume rests on his being the master of the young John Wootton.

Coll: Ipswich and Nottingham A.G's and in the Mellon Collection.

Illustration in B.S.P.

XAVERY, J. op. 1772-1798

This cattle-painter exhibited his work in London during these years.

It is not known if and how he was related to Jacob Xavery of the Hague, born in 1736, or his brother Gerard Joseph Xavery, who, between them, painted historical subjects, landscapes, sea-ports, fruit, and flowers.

YOUNG, T. op. 1788

Grant records 'A Horse in a Landscape' of this date by this painter.

ZUTSAL, D. G. op. 19th century

The influence of this Continental painter, who was at work in England in the 19th century, was widespread. Examples indicate that he reached the bottom of the treacle-barrel of Victorian sentimentality: no more need be said.

1. Oil   JACQUES LAURENT AGASSE.   1767-1849
The Nubian Giraffe
By gracious permission of H.M. the Queen

2. Oil   RICHARD ANSDELL, R.A. 1815-1885 $29\frac{1}{4}$ x 60 in.
The Tired Sheep
Courtesy, Frost & Reed Ltd, Bristol & London

3. Oil   BESSIE BAMBER
Kittens
Courtesy, Oscar & Peter Johnson Ltd, London

4. Oil

FRANCIS BARLOW. *c.* 1626-1704
Coursing
Courtesy, The Tryon Gallery, London

5. Oil THOMAS BLINKS. 1860-1912 20 x 30 in.
Shooting Scene. S. & D. 1890
Courtesy, Richard Green Fine Paintings, London

6. Oil   E. E. BREACH.   op. 1868-1886 $28\frac{1}{2}$ x $48\frac{1}{2}$ in.
                         A Tempting Dish.   S. & D. 1878
                    Courtesy, Richard Green Fine Paintings, London

7. Oil   E. BROWN.   op. 1840-1857
Dogs
Courtesy, The Parker Gallery, London

8.   WILLIAM FRANK CALDERON, R.I.   1865-1943
Sketch of a Fox Hound
Author's collection

9.   **ROBERT CLEMINSON.** op. 1865-1901
'Sovereign of the Hill'
Courtesy, Oscar & Peter Johnson Ltd, London

10. Oil   THOMAS SIDNEY COOPER, R.A.   1803-1902   42 x 64 in.
                        Sheep and Goats by a Highland Loch
                        Courtesy, Williams & Son, London

11. Oil   HORATIO H. COULDERY.   1832-1893   22 x 33 in.

'The Intruder'

Courtesy, Spenser S.A., London

12.   JOSEPH CRAWHALL.   1861-1913 $35\frac{3}{4}$ x 50 in.
A Lincolnshire Pasture
In the City Art Gallery, Dundee

13. Oil   J. DUNN.   op. 1840-1851   25 x 33 in.

Fat Shorthorn Ox in a Landscape

Courtesy, Frost & Reed Ltd, Bristol & London

14. Oil   MAUD EARL.   op. 1884-1919 $17\frac{1}{2}$ x 23 in.
'Japanese Fine Feathers'
Courtesy, Richard Green Fine Paintings, London

15. Oil

JOHN COLIN EDWARDS.   1940 - living
Badgers at Dusk
Courtesy, The Moorland Gallery, London

18. Oil   GEORGE CHRISTOPHER HORNER.   1829-1881
Macomo and Friends
Courtesy, Michael Parkin Fine Art Ltd, London

19. Oil   **WILLIAM HUGGINS.**   1820-1884   16 x 22 in.
Lion at Rest. S. & D. 1865
Courtesy, Oscar & Peter Jackson Ltd, London

20. Oil   **EDGAR HUNT.**   *c.* 1873-1955   20 x 30 in.
A Happy Family.   S. & D. 1907
Courtesy, Richard Green Fine Paintings, London

21. Oil   LOUIS B. HURT.   1859-1929   20 x 30 in.
Mists of the Morning
Courtesy, Williams & Son, London

22. Oil   **CHARLES JONES.**   1836-1892   14 x 20 in.

Sheep and Lambs

Courtesy, B. Cohen & Sons, London

23. Oil   SIR EDWIN LANDSEER, R.A.   1802-1873
Otter Hounds
Courtesy, The Tryon Gallery Ltd, London

24. Oil   SIR EDWIN LANDSEER, R.A.   1802-1873 $14\frac{1}{2}$ x $17\frac{1}{2}$ in.
Puppy Teasing a Frog
In the Harris Museum & Art Gallery, Preston

25. Water-colour   **EDWARD LEAR.** 1812-1888
Kangaroo. S. & D. 1837
In a private collection. Photo courtesy, Gooden & Fox, London

26. Oil   LUCY LEAVERS. op. 1887-1898   34 x 48 in.

The Antagonist

Courtesy, W. H. Patterson, London

27. Oil   ROBERT NIGHTINGALE.   1815-1895   12 x 20 in.

Rex II – Champion Gordon Setter. S. & D. 1881

Courtesy, Spenser S.A., London

28. Oil   JAMES NORTHCOTE, R.A.   1746-1831 $39\frac{1}{4}$ x $49\frac{3}{4}$ in.
Mother and Cubs
Courtesy, Leva Gallery, London

29. Oil   BENJAMIN CAM NORTON.   op. 1862-1890
Three Cats
Courtesy, Michael Parkin Fine Art Ltd, London

30. Oil   **ROBERT PHYSICK, R.B.A.**   op. 1859-1866   20 x 23 in.
Farmyard with Goat and Kids
Courtesy, Spenser S.A., London

31. Oil   DAVID SHEPHERD.   1931 - living   22 x 30 in.
Young Greater Kudu
Courtesy, The Tryon Gallery Ltd, London

32. Oil   GEORGE STUBBS, A.R.A.   1724-1806
The Green Monkey
In the Walker Art Gallery, Liverpool

33. Oil   AGNES AUGUSTA TALBOYS, R.W.A.   1863-1941   17 x 28 in.
'Coquetry'
Courtesy, Frost & Reed Ltd, Bristol & London

34.
RALPH THOMPSON
Serval Kittens
Courtesy, The Tryon Gallery Ltd, London

35.   **ARCHIBALD THORBURN.**   1860-1935
A Long-tailed Field Mouse and a Yellow-necked Mouse. S. & D. 1903
Courtesy, The McDonald Booth Gallery, London

36.   **WILLIAM TIMYM.** 1912 - living
Caracal – Head Study
Courtesy, The Moorland Gallery, London

37. Oil   T. UNDERWOOD.   op. *c.* 1844-1849 $24\frac{1}{2}$ x $30\frac{1}{4}$ in.

Roan and White Shorthorn Bull

Courtesy, Frost & Reed Ltd, Bristol & London

38. Oil   JAMES WARD, R.A.   1769-1859
                         'Buff' a Poodle.   S. & D. 1812
                    Courtesy, Frank Partridge & Son, Ltd, London

39. Oil   ARTHUR WARDLE, R.I.   1864-1949
Tigers
Courtesy, Oscar & Peter Johnson Ltd, London

40. Oil   **THOMAS WEAVER.**   1774-1843
Cows
Courtesy, Frost & Reed Ltd, Bristol & London

41. Oil   WILLIAM WEEKES. op. 1864-1904
Two Donkeys and Hens
Courtesy, Oscar & Peter Johnson Ltd, London

42. Water-colour   **WILLIAM WOODHOUSE.**   1857-1939 $10\frac{3}{4}$ x $15\frac{1}{8}$ in.

Snow Leopard

In the Harris Museum & Art Gallery, Preston